W9-BCS-080

THE EVERYTHING

Baby Sign
Language Book

Dear Reader,

The first time I witnessed baby sign language in action, my son was just two months old, and crying, cooing, and smiling were the only ways in which he could communicate. So when I watched another mother speak with her infant son in a way that I couldn't, I was intrigued. I immediately went out and did research on baby sign language. I discovered its benefits, and I learned how to demonstrate it to a baby. Four months later, my son signed MILK to me for the first time. I was hooked. Since then, we have learned dozens of new signs together.

There is something magical about signing with a baby. It gives you a glimpse into the workings of his little mind and provides extra insight into his personality. It is nothing short of amazing. As you embark upon your own signing journey, it is my sincere hope that you, too, will delight in communicating with your baby in this special way.

Sincerely,

Teresa R. Simpson

Welcome to the EVERYTHING Series!

These handy, accessible books give you all you need to tackle a difficult project, gain a new hobby, comprehend a fascinating topic, prepare for an exam, or even brush up on something you learned back in school but have since forgotten.

You can choose to read an *Everything*® book from cover to cover or just pick out the information you want from our four useful boxes: e-questions, e-facts, e-alerts, e-ssentials. We give you everything you need to know on the subject, but throw in a lot of fun stuff along the way, too.

We now have more than 400 *Everything*® books in print, spanning such wide-ranging categories as weddings, pregnancy, cooking, music instruction, foreign language, crafts, pets, New Age, and so much more. When you're done reading them all, you can finally say you know *Everything*®!

E-QUESTION	E-FACT	E-ALERT	E-SSENTIAL
Answers to common questions	Important snippets of information	Urgent warnings	Quick handy tips

DIRECTOR OF INNOVATION Paula Munier

EDITORIAL DIRECTOR Laura M. Daly

EXECUTIVE EDITOR, SERIES BOOKS Brielle K. Matson

ASSOCIATE COPY CHIEF Sheila Zwiebel

ACQUISITIONS EDITOR Brielle K. Matson

DEVELOPMENT EDITOR Brett Palana-Shanahan

PRODUCTION EDITOR Casey Ebert

Visit the entire Everything® series at *www.everything.com*

THE EVERYTHING

BABY SIGN LANGUAGE BOOK

with DVD

Get an early start communicating with your baby!

Teresa R. Simpson

Technical Review by Terrell Clark, Ph.D.

Avon, Massachusetts

For the men in my life, Michael and James, with all my love.

Copyright © 2008 by F+W Publications, Inc. All rights reserved.
This book, or parts thereof, may not be reproduced
in any form without permission from the publisher; exceptions
are made for brief excerpts used in published reviews.

An Everything® Series Book.
Everything® and everything.com® are registered trademarks of F+W Publications, Inc.

Published by Adams Media, an F+W Publications Company
57 Littlefield Street, Avon, MA 02322 U.S.A.
www.adamsmedia.com

ISBN 10: 1-59869-564-9
ISBN 13: 978-1-59869-564-9

Printed in the United States of America.

J   I   H   G   F   E   D   C   B   A

Library of Congress Cataloging-in-Publication Data
is available from the publisher.

This publication is designed to provide accurate and authoritative information with regard to the subject matter covered. It is sold with the understanding that the publisher is not engaged in rendering legal, accounting, or other professional advice. If legal advice or other expert assistance is required, the services of a competent professional person should be sought.

   —From a *Declaration of Principles* jointly adopted by a Committee of the American Bar Association and a Committee of Publishers and Associations

Many of the designations used by manufacturers and sellers to distinguish their products are claimed as trademarks. Where those designations appear in this book and Adams Media was aware of a trademark claim, the designations have been printed with initial capital letters.

This book is available at quantity discounts for bulk purchases.
For information, please call 1-800-289-0963.

Contents

Getting Started / 65

Signs for Baby's First Needs / 77

Signs for Parts of Baby's Day / 91

Signs for the People in Baby's World / 101

CONTENTS

14   Around the House Signs / 151

15   Signs of the Great Outdoors / 163

16   Transportation Signs / 175

Signs for Concepts / 185

Signs of Feelings and Affection / 199

Troubleshooting Common Problems / 211

Now That Baby Is Signing / 221

Top Ten Reasons to Sign with Your Baby

1. Your baby is trying to tell you something!
2. You will learn to sign right along with your baby.
3. Signing is a fun activity for the whole family.
4. Your baby will experience less frustration as she gets her needs met.
5. Less frustration for your baby means less frustration for you!
6. Your baby will be able to communicate with other signing babies.
7. Signing promotes interaction between you and your baby.
8. Babies who sign are better able to express themselves appropriately.
9. Signing provides the basis for a second "language" as your child gets older.
10. Babies who sign often score higher on IQ tests later in life than their nonsigning peers.

Introduction

▶ USING SIGN LANGUAGE to communicate with babies—it seems like everybody's doing it. Okay, maybe not *everybody,* but certainly many people are doing it, and their numbers seem to increase with each passing year. A few years ago, you might have encountered an occasional hearing mom on the playground signing with her hearing baby. Such a mom (or dad) typically would have been thought of as an over-achiever trying to raise a super-baby. Today, however, parents by the thousands are discovering the immense benefits of signing with their babies, and they are learning that a signing baby is not the same as a super-baby. It is no longer uncommon to see young children signing with their parents, their siblings, and even with their caregivers in day-care settings. In fact, because of the increased prevalence of baby sign, babies are now signing with each other.

So what prompted this sudden popularity of baby sign language? Is it a trendy fad that will lose steam over the next few years? Signing parents will assure you that this is not the case. Instead, it is a major advancement in the field of baby communication. Baby sign language opens up a whole new world of communication between a baby and the adults around her. It allows parents to gain early insight into the way her mind works, and it bridges the communication gap that exists during her preverbal months. Something this powerful is unlikely to go away. Instead, it seems likely that more and more parents will get onboard the baby-signing train and that it will eventually become a widespread and common practice.

Signing is a beautiful way to communicate with your child. It is fun and educational, and it is an excellent way to spend quality time together. In addition to the communication advantages it provides, signing can also contribute to a child's academic prowess, as well as to her self-esteem. Best of all, it is an activity in which the whole family can participate.

If you are reading this book, you are undoubtedly interested in learning how to sign with your baby. You may know a lot or a little about the subject. You may wonder how it is done or where to begin. You may be familiar with sign language, or you may be a complete novice. You may still be skeptical that baby sign is even possible. The good news is that this book will address every one of these scenarios and more. You will learn how baby sign language works, why it works, and how to use it with your baby.

This book and DVD set will also show you how to make almost 200 signs. On the DVD, you will find a demonstration of each and every sign. An explanation of each sign is also included in the book. Dispersed throughout the book, you will also find photographs depicting the simpler signs that do not need in-depth illustration.

Congratulations on making the choice to sign! It is a beautiful gift to give to your child and to yourself. As you set out on your signing journey, prepare to be amazed by the things your baby wants to tell you, and prepare to watch her personality shine through in ways you have not yet imagined. Successful signing takes time and patience, but it is worth the wait.

Acknowledgments

I would like to thank Brielle Matson for giving me the opportunity to share my knowledge of baby sign language. Her patience and guidance has made this a pleasurable experience. I would also like to acknowledge the assistance of William G. Vicars, Ed.D., whose sign language expertise was instrumental to the writing of this book.

A special thank you goes to my parents and sisters—Foster, Susan, Sally, and Audrey Bunday—for their lifelong encouragement and support. And finally, I wish to thank my in-laws—Ruth and Jack Smith, James Simpson, and Tonya Young—for taking care of my "boys" for several days while I finished this book.

Chapter 1

Why Sign with Your Baby?

The benefits of signing with your baby are numerous. In addition to the developmental advantages it brings, parents and caregivers love being able to interact with their children. In this chapter, find out why sign language is the "new" language being spoken in playgroups, parks, and day-care centers across the country and how easy it is for you and your child to acquire.

Signing Is Fun and Easy

If you are new to baby sign language, you may feel a bit overwhelmed and unsure of where to start. You may wonder if you are actually capable of signing with your baby and what to expect when and if she masters the signs. The good news is that it takes no special skills to sign with your baby, nor does a baby require great aptitude to acquire sign language. If you practice sign language frequently and consistently, you can expect your baby to experience these three basic stages of the learning process:

- First, she will begin to take notice while you sign.
- Next, she will imitate your signs.
- Finally, she will attach meaning to signs and use them to communicate.

You may also be concerned that the process will be a time-consuming chore or that you will have to push your baby hard in order to make progress. Fortunately, learning sign language does not have to be difficult. It is easily incorporated into everyday life and quickly becomes a habit. In addition, most of the signs that you will be practicing with your baby are basic and simple to form. Both parent and baby usually remember them easily.

Not only can signing be simple, it can (and should) be fun for everyone involved. Signing lessons can be turned into a game or can accompany a song. There are plenty of suggestions in Chapter 20 for keeping it fun, but you and your baby will likely come up with your own fun ways to learn to sign.

Meaningful Conversation

As the parent or caregiver of a baby, you have undoubtedly spent a great deal of time in one-sided conversation. With very little response from your little one, it can be difficult to know how much, if any, of the conversation she comprehends. On the flip side of that conundrum is the likelihood that your baby has also engaged in some one-sided conversations of her own. She may coo, babble, or use baby jargon. She may be trying to express her needs or just chatting about the world around her.

While you and your baby won't engage in fluent sign-language conversations, you will find that the level of communication that sign language provides will change your life in a positive and noticeable way. The use of sign opens up a whole new expressive world for the two of you and gives you the ability to engage in far more meaningful conversation than you are otherwise able to have.

E-FACT

Cooing is usually one of a baby's earliest attempts at communication. Babies as young as two months of age often make "ooh" and "ahh" sounds. These adorable little noises are often her first efforts at making conversation and should be responded to as such.

Less Frustration for Baby

As babies become more expressive, they also become more frustrated when they are unable to convey their thoughts, wants, or needs. They are doing all they can to be clear, yet they can't seem to get anyone to understand them. This communication gap can lead to temper tantrums, crying jags, and a feeling of dissatisfaction. As your baby begins to acquire some basic signs, she will discover that signing can get a response from you that crying and "talking" doesn't always bring. This will result in a happier baby who derives a great deal of satisfaction from being understood.

Less Frustration for You

It surely goes without saying that a happier baby results in a happier parent. As baby's frustration is diminished due to her newfound ability to communicate, you will find that her improved mood will greatly improve yours, as well. But the benefits don't end there. In the same way that baby gets frustrated when she can't get her point across to you, you likely feel a certain amount of frustration when you are unable to convey your message to her. As your baby begins to understand your signs, you will begin to see the communication gap narrowing. Of course, a baby understands your spoken word long before she begins to speak, but when you are able to use signs that she herself is able to use, you will know with certainty that she comprehends what you are saying to her.

Help for the Terrible Twos

If you are looking for a surefire quick fix for the terrible twos, you will not find it through sign language. The terrible twos are a developmental must, and every child goes through them. The good news is that improved communication between you and your baby can result in a less intense terrible-twos phase. The reason for this is that the terrible twos are the result of baby's growing independence. She wants to assert that independence and make choices and decisions on her own. Unfortunately, you will not be able to give in to her every whim, and tantrums will still ensue. However, her ability to communicate through the use of sign will reduce the number of tantrums because she will be able to express her choices to you.

E-ALERT

If you think that you won't have to start dealing with temper tantrums until your baby is two years old, think again. The term *terrible twos* is a misnomer: This developmental stage often begins when a child is just a year old and may last until she is three.

For instance, a toddler might be able to tell you that she wants to eat. So you offer her a piece of fruit, a cracker, or another snack. Much to your dismay, however, your toddler begins crying, screaming, or stomping in protest. Why? Because you aren't offering her what she wants, and because of her independent streak, she will not be satisfied with anything else. A baby who is able to sign, however, can tell you that what she *really* wants is a slice of cheese or a cookie. The terrible twos will reign on, but thanks to the use of sign language, they won't be quite so bad.

Does Signing Make Babies Smarter?

Does the thought of a signing baby bring to mind images of those super-babies who can speak four languages and play the piano by the time they're eighteen months old? If so, you're not alone. Many people mistakenly believe that sign language is something that only overachieving parents would use with their kids. The fact is that babies who sign generally *do* have some developmental and academic advantages over their nonsigning peers. Does this mean you are pushing your child to be a genius or demanding super-intelligence from your toddler? Of course not. It simply means that you are giving your child an invaluable advantage that has multiple benefits.

Higher IQ Potential

Studies performed by researchers at the National Institutes of Health have indicated that babies who learn to sign end up with higher IQs as they get older. While there may be some merit to this finding, it is also important to remember the other factors involved. Parents who sign with their babies are typically very involved in their children's academic development. They may place a heavy emphasis on education and may often be intellectuals, themselves. They are likely to have studied all sorts of ways to give their children advantages from nutrition to educational experiences. All of these factors can help to contribute to higher IQs. Does this mean that learning sign language does not improve IQ scores later in life? Not at all! It's just worth noting that there are many reasons why a signing baby may grow up to be generally intelligent.

Improved Self-Expression

Another important benefit of baby sign language is that signing babies are better able to express themselves in all sorts of ways. That is, they are able to convey their thoughts and feelings in a way that nonsigning babies cannot. This ability may result in babies who are more confident and out-spoken. They may come to understand the validity of their feelings earlier and understand that it is acceptable to express them.

The Multilingual Baby

Research studies at the University of Washington have proven that it can be beneficial to teach a baby more than one language. Babies are better able to learn a second (or third) language than older children and adults. As they get older, children who are multilingual have an easier time adding additional languages to their repertoires. Being multilingual also gives them a better understanding of language in general, which could lead to better reading, writing, and comprehension skills.

> ## E-QUESTION
>
> *Can my baby acquire sign language in a home that is already bilingual?*
>
> Yes. Many bilingual families have discovered that sign language actually improves their child's comprehension of each of the home's spoken languages by providing a common denominator.

American Sign Language (ASL) is a language all its own. For that reason, a baby who is taught ASL will enjoy many of the same benefits of a child who speaks two or more spoken languages, particularly if she continues to develop her signing skills into childhood. Even if you choose to use "home signs," your child will still reap many of the same benefits. See Chapter 3 for information on the different methods of sign language instruction and to decide which method is right for you and your child.

Bonding with Baby

Whenever you spend one-on-one time with your baby, you are helping to create a bond that will last a lifetime. Bonding is something that happens not in an hour or a day but rather through repeated sessions of quality time. Signing with your child is one way to add a little bonding time into your routine. It provides an opportunity to learn together and engage in conversation with one another.

Quality Time

Families today are often so busy that they don't have much opportunity for quality time. Meals are eaten in a rush, music is only listened to in the car, and the television is a willing babysitter when a parent needs a few minutes to attend to another task. Because of this constant rushing around, many people fail to enjoy the moments spent with their children, as they are looking ahead to the next thing that has to be done.

Using sign language with your child, however, helps you to focus on the task at hand. If, during dinner, you are busy demonstrating the signs for CHICKEN and PEAS and FORK, you will be focusing on your meal and, more importantly, on your child. She will enjoy the interaction, and you will find that your mealtime is more enjoyable.

Security, Without the Blanket

There are many things in baby's world that can offer her a sense of security. A cherished blanket, a familiar story, and a well-loved teddy bear can all be of comfort to a baby or young child. There is nothing, however, that offers her more comfort and security than her parent or other full-time caregiver.

E-SSENTIAL

Because many babies often form such a strong attachment to transitional objects like blankets, pillows, and teddy bears, these are good early signs to introduce. A baby will be delighted to discover that she can ask for the item simply by forming the sign. This will motivate her to form the sign again and again.

This feeling of security develops as a baby learns that she can depend on you to meet all of her needs. Through signing, you will be able to provide for even more of her needs because you will better understand her requests. The more signing you and your baby do together, the better your responses to her needs will be, thus increasing your baby's sense of security.

Instant Camaraderie

Do you remember being a child and forming a secret club with your friends? Perhaps you and your friends developed a special code that only you and they were able to understand. These special things held only between you and your friends gave you a sense of closeness that you would not have had ordinarily. The same is true for you and your baby when you practice sign together. Think of it as a special language between you and your baby. It is amazing to be able to communicate with your child in a way that others can't. The two of you are likely to build a deeper friendship with this shared language that can last a lifetime.

When your baby first begins to sign, she will likely try out her signing skills with everyone around her, and she may grow frustrated when she discovers that not everyone responds to her signs. She will soon figure out who can understand her and who can't. Those who can will enjoy sharing this special language with your child.

A Skill to Last a Lifetime

The most obvious and immediate benefit of signing with your baby is improved communication. But a child who is taught American Sign Language signs (ASL) can retain this skill into childhood and beyond. Of course, a baby or toddler will not become fluent in American Sign Language, just as she will not be fluent in spoken English until she is older. However, baby sign (just like baby talk) can be the foundation that your child builds upon. A child who has acquired the basics of sign language as a baby will be a step ahead of ASL beginners.

E-FACT

Prepubescent children are able to develop a fluency in a second or third language that is comparable to native speakers of the language. Older children and adults usually cannot. This makes infancy and early childhood an ideal time to introduce a second language, including sign.

Keep in mind that sign language is not just for babies. If you have an older child in the house, he can benefit, too. You can start out by demonstrating to him the same signs that you use with your baby (though obviously an older child might not have much use for words such as "bottle" and "diaper"). Unlike your baby, your older child will be able to learn the signs very quickly. In fact, don't be surprised if your older child breezes through the signs in this book in just a matter of weeks. If he seems to be hungry for more signing opportunities, you might want to enroll him in a sign language class. This will help him to learn the patterns, rhythms, and rules of American Sign Language.

Dispelling Common Myths

As with anything else in life that is misunderstood, a few myths seem to rear their ugly heads over and over in regard to baby sign language. Here are a few:

- Babies who sign are slower to talk.
- Babies who sign are being pushed too hard.
- Sign language can be confusing for a baby.
- Babies can't really sign.

E-SSENTIAL

As a signing parent, it is important that you believe in what you are doing. This will help to keep you and your child motivated. If you find that you are having doubts about the validity or effectiveness of baby sign language, talk to other signing parents and listen to their insight and experiences.

As you will read in the following sections, all of these myths can be easily refuted. If you find that family, friends, and strangers keep bringing up these misconceptions, see Chapter 5 for advice on dealing with criticism and skepticism.

Myth: Slower to Talk

The idea that babies who sign are slower to talk than their nonsigning peers is one that comes from the misunderstanding that sign language actually replaces the spoken word. For babies who are able to hear, that just is not true. In fact, babies who practice sign language are often quicker to talk than their nonsigning peers. Why? Because part of using signs with babies involves saying each word out loud as you are signing. For this reason, many signing babies will learn a new spoken word and its sign at the same time.

Myth: Pushed Too Hard

Many people who are uneducated about baby sign language feel that these babies are being pushed too hard to learn a skill that is outside of their natural ability. These nay-sayers liken baby sign language to things like trying to teach a baby how to play concert piano or do long division.

E-ALERT

Although a parent who signs with her baby is not necessarily trying to create a super-baby, it is possible to subject her to undue amounts of pressure. This is true for any skill a baby is learning, such as walking, talking, or potty training. Remember to be patient with your child and let her learn at her own pace.

The truth is, babies have a natural inclination to gesture and do so on their own to express their needs. Babies will raise their arms when they want to be picked up and point to an object that they want to have. Using sign language just taps into this natural ability.

Myth: Confusion for Baby

Subscribers to this myth believe that signing with babies will be confusing because they will not understand what you are saying. In the beginning, of course, they will not understand, just as they do not understand an unfamiliar new word the first time you speak it. However, as you continue to sign with your baby, comprehension will set in. When that happens, your baby will likely be less confused by language than her nonsigning peers.

Myth: Babies Can't Sign

It goes without saying that those who believe a baby can't learn to sign are people who have never witnessed it for themselves. These unbelievers may think that a baby is just making meaningless gestures or that a parent is seeing something that isn't really there. Unfortunately, these skeptics will not be convinced until they see a signing baby in action. There are thousands of signing babies and toddlers whose signing skills could easily prove that babies *can* sign. It won't be long before your baby can prove it, too!

Chapter 2

Why Signing Works

If you are new to the world of baby sign language, you may be wondering if babies can really use sign. Scientific studies conducted by baby-sign pioneers, such as Dr. Joseph Garcia and Dr. Linda Acredolo, have shown that they can. More importantly, though, babies across the country are proving it by actually using sign language to communicate with those around them. This chapter will explore the reasons why sign language works for countless others and why it can also work for you and your baby.

Traditional Use of Sign

In its infancy, structured sign language was developed as a method for Deaf people to communicate with each other. In one form or another, it has been in practice for many years. In fact, one of the founding fathers of sign language was a sixteenth-century Italian physician named Geronimo Cardano. He developed the notion that Deaf people could learn to communicate by using a standard set of symbols. Until the late 1950s, however, the use of sign language was a controversial subject, and not everyone saw it as a legitimate form of communication. For years, sign language was banned even in schools for the Deaf. This was done in an attempt to mainstream children who were deaf or hard of hearing.

Today, sign language is widely used and accepted but is still considered to be the method of communication used primarily by the Deaf and hard of hearing. Certainly, the Deaf and hard of hearing make up the largest portion of signers, but sign language can be used by *anyone* with speech limitations to communicate with others. The Deaf, the mute, the developmentally challenged, and those with speech delays or handicaps all use sign language.

E-FACT

Statistics published by the National Institute on Deafness and Other Communication Disorders indicate that approximately 28 million Americans have some sort of hearing impairment and that two to three out of every 1,000 children in the United States are born deaf or hard of hearing.

All young babies, regardless of their hearing capabilities, are unable to speak for the first few months of their lives. On average, babies do not speak their first words until around twelve months of age (though any time from nine months to fifteen months of age is considered within normal limits). Babies will not begin to construct simple sentences of two to three words until at least eighteen months of age. In fact, many toddlers are nearly three before they have a well-established command of the English language. This lack of communication can be frustrating for both the baby and his parents. Fortunately, however, babies typically have more control over their hands than they do over their speech. If their gesturing skills are cultivated, they can use this control to communicate long before they are able to speak.

Though sign language has been around for hundreds of years, it has only been in the last twenty years or so that baby sign language has grown in popularity. Even more recently, baby sign language has become almost trendy. As more and more families continue to discover the immense benefits that signing provides to their babies, baby sign language may someday be viewed as a traditional, legitimate, and even a common use of sign.

Research on Sign Language for Babies

Research on baby sign language as it relates to babies without hearing impairments has been limited, primarily because it is a newer practice. The research that has been done, however, has shown that the use of sign language can offer tremendous benefits to hearing babies. This research, conducted by a few prominent investigators in the field of baby sign language, has shaped the way that many parents think about signing with their babies.

Dr. Joseph Garcia's Research

One of the pioneers of baby sign language, Dr. Joseph Garcia, first considered the possibility of using sign with babies who are not deaf when he was working as a sign-language interpreter. He observed that the hearing babies of deaf parents were able to communicate by signing earlier than their nonsigning peers who had hearing parents. For these babies, sign language was simply a second language "spoken" within their homes. Long before their verbal skills had developed, they were using signs to express their needs. Armed with this knowledge, Dr. Garcia began to explore the benefits of signing with the hearing babies of hearing parents. He discovered that if taught consistently, starting at about six months of age, these babies could begin to sign by the time they were eight or nine months old.

Drs. Linda Acredolo and Susan Goodwyn and Their Research

Two other prominent researchers in the field, Dr. Linda Acredolo and Dr. Susan Goodwyn, conducted extensive studies on sign language for hearing babies. Their research indicated that signing babies went on to have a better command of the English language, with larger vocabularies and longer sentences as toddlers, than their nonsigning peers. In addition, the signing babies were given IQ tests at eight years of age. On average, these children scored twelve points higher than did other children their age.

E-SSENTIAL

Before you put too much emphasis on your child's IQ, it is important to know that approximately half of the population has an IQ in the *average* range of 90 to 110. It is further estimated that 25 percent of the population has an IQ below 90 and the remaining 25 percent has a score above 110.

It is interesting to note that Drs. Acredolo and Goodwyn are proponents of symbolic gestures, otherwise known as *home signs,* while Dr. Garcia advocates the use of American Sign Language. This would suggest that both methods are effective and beneficial to babies. The next chapter will examine the various methods associated with baby sign language, as well as the advantages and drawbacks of each method.

Babies with Special Developmental Needs

If you are the parent of a baby with special developmental needs, you may wonder if your child is capable of learning sign. You might be surprised to know that sign language has been taught to many babies with astounding results. The severity and nature of a child's limitations will determine whether or not he is capable of learning sign language. It is encouraging to note, however, that numerous parents have been successful in demonstrating sign language to children with a wide array of conditions.

Many conditions can result in speech delays, but some of the most common include apraxia of speech, autism, Down syndrome, prematurity, and specific language impairment. If your child has been diagnosed with any of these conditions, you will likely find it encouraging to know that many other children with the same conditions do extraordinarily well with sign language and are often better communicators than their nonsigning peers.

E-ALERT

Because most children do not experience significant leaps in speech development until they are eighteen months old, delays in speech cannot be accurately assessed until a child is between eighteen and twenty-four months of age. However, it is important to mention concerns you have about your child at *any* age to your child's pediatrician.

Apraxia of Speech

Apraxia of speech (also known as verbal apraxia, verbal dyspraxia, or developmental apraxia of speech) is a somewhat common neurological speech disorder in which a child (or person of any age) is unable to consistently voice his thoughts intelligibly. It has been found that children who have this condition are usually quite capable of understanding spoken language even if they are unable to express themselves. Because of this comprehension, children with apraxia of speech can often learn to use sign language to effectively communicate.

Autism

Autism is an extremely common disorder. According to the U.S. Centers for Disease Control, autism affects one out of 150 people, most commonly boys. People with autism have difficulty communicating and relating socially with other people. Other common behavior traits in individuals with autism are repetitive behaviors or strict adherence to routines. Generally, autism can be accurately diagnosed by the time a child is three years old; however, diagnoses can sometimes be made much earlier. Because autism greatly affects a child's ability to communicate, a child who has autism may benefit from the use of sign language.

Down Syndrome

Down syndrome is a well-recognized and somewhat common condition. The National Down Syndrome Society estimates that the condition occurs in one in 733 live births. Down syndrome is usually associated with some degree of mental retardation, meaning that children who have the condition learn and develop at a slower pace than their peers.

> ## E-FACT
>
> Contrary to some beliefs, studies have proven that children (including those with Down syndrome) will stop using signs once they can express themselves effectively through speech. That is, when others begin to understand your child, your child will no longer need to use signs. Of course, you can encourage the use of signs for as long as you wish after that.

In spite of their delayed development, children with Down syndrome are often creative communicators. Though they may have difficulty speaking, they frequently use gestures and animated facial expressions to express themselves. This natural inclination to communicate with their hands and face makes these children ideal candidates for sign language.

Prematurity

When a baby is born prematurely, his developmental progress is usually measured not by his chronological age but by his adjusted age. A child's adjusted age is the age he would be had he been born full-term. For instance, a baby who was two months premature will have an adjusted age of six months when he reaches eight months of age. This means that his skills will likely be on par with an average six-month-old instead of an eight-month-old. Because speech is one of the skills that may be delayed in the premature infant, sign language can be of tremendous benefit to the preemie and his family.

Specific Language Impairment

Specific language impairment (SLI) is a common but somewhat vague disorder. The degree of incidence varies from one age to another. A University of Kansas study revealed that SLI effects between 7 and 8 percent of children who are kindergarten age. Children with SLI may have normal or above-average intelligence. Although SLI does not have any effect on hearing, sign language is one way in which to help bridge the communication gap for children with this disorder.

Naturally Speaking

Babies communicate in a variety of ways from the moment they are born. The youngest of babies will connect with his parents both by crying and by making eye contact. This most primitive of exchanges enables a baby to express his needs or displeasure and also allows him to bond with his parents.

As a baby gets older, his methods of communication become more sophisticated. He graduates to coos and smiles to express his contentment, and his cries become distinctive to his needs. At this time, he is probably discovering the many amazing things that he can do with his hands. This skill will come in handy soon.

E-SSENTIAL

Even though a baby as young as two months has probably already discovered his hands, he is not yet quite ready to sign. Although it is fine to demonstrate signs at any age, a baby this young does not have the dexterity to sign, nor is he able to make connections between an object and its sign.

When a baby nears toddlerhood, his growing independence makes him work harder to get his point across. It is important to him that he is able to express himself, and it is equally important that you respond appropriately. He will begin to be more adamant with his verbal sounds and babbles and will begin to gesture with his hands. Commonly, he will point to things that he wants or raise his arms to be picked up.

Baby See, Baby Do

Imitation may be the sincerest form of flattery, but it is also an important learning tool for babies. Even very young infants will mimic mouth movements. As a baby gets older, he finds that imitating his parents usually earns him a favorable response. This fuels his fire and encourages him to continue mimicking you.

As you sign with your baby, he will be presented with many opportunities to imitate you. In fact, there may be some signs that he forms before he comprehends their meaning, simply because he wants to do what you are doing. This desire to imitate is one reason why babies tend to pick up sign language so easily.

As your baby gets older, he will be more aware of the world around him, and he will begin to watch all the people he sees. Soon he will begin to imitate those people, as well, particularly if he sees them often or is especially drawn to them. This is why it is so important to get everyone involved in the signing process.

Because of your baby's tendency to imitate, it is important that you model the signs as accurately as possible. Even if you feel yourself getting frustrated or feel that your child is not paying attention, model them correctly anyway. You never know when your little imitator will start signing.

Everybody's Doing It

Scientific research aside, babies everywhere are proving that they are capable of using sign language. This growing trend is apparent in the sheer number of classes and materials that are available on the subject. An Internet search on "baby sign language" will return thousands of hits, and the practice has also received attention from popular parenting guides. Baby sign language has even made its way into pop culture, a fact made evident by the movie *Meet the Fockers*. In this film, Robert De Niro's character is practicing sign language with his one-year-old grandson.

E-FACT

Baby sign language isn't just making an appearance in works of Hollywood fiction. Celebrities like Debra Messing and Julia Roberts are signing with their own children and are becoming advocates of the practice. Due to their fame and frequent public appearances, signing celebrities are spreading the word about baby sign language.

The reason that signing is becoming so popular is not because it is a trendy thing to do. Instead, its popularity is a clear indication that sign language is working for many babies and their families. Additionally, it is worth noting that this popularity is not limited to large metropolitan areas. Families all over the country, in both big cities and tiny towns, are practicing sign with their babies.

Because the practice is so widespread, you will probably be able to find other signers in your community. This will provide you with a network of support to share with you in the joys and frustrations that accompany signing. Not only will you benefit, but your baby will, too. He will enjoy having other babies with whom he can sign, and you will take great delight in watching these early conversations take place.

If you are unable to find signing families in your area, do not let that stop you from developing friendships with other signers. Use the Internet to find signing message boards, chat rooms, and e-mail lists. The friendships you make online can be just as fulfilling as those you make in real life and will often provide just as much support.

Chapter 3

The Schools of Sign

From the structure of American Sign Language (ASL) to the flexibility of home signs, there are several different methods used when signing with babies. Unfortunately, everyone seems to have a different opinion on which method is best. If you are not sure which one is right for you, keep reading. This chapter examines the different methods and the benefits and shortcomings of each to help you make an informed decision.

Which Method Is Best?

If you are new to the concept of baby sign language, you might not even realize that there *are* different methods available to you. In fact, you probably assumed that sign language for babies is no different than sign language for adults. Fortunately for you and signing parents everywhere, this is not the case. Adults who are fluent in sign have mastered a complete second language. Even if you choose to use ASL, your baby will only be using basic signs. After all, a baby who has yet to master her native language will certainly find it difficult to acquire a second language.

If you opt to use what are known as *home signs* or *baby gestures,* then you will actually be using made-up signs that may be unlike ASL. If those options aren't enough, there are combinations of the two and other variations that some parents opt to use. As with ASL, these other methods only require that your baby learn basic words and perhaps simple phrases.

E-SSENTIAL

To get a good look at these methods in practice, visit a baby sign language class or playgroup, many of which will welcome you as an investigator of baby sign. Witnessing signing babies and their parents in action will give you an idea of what to expect from each technique.

The decision of which method is best seems to be a matter of perspective. It is important to remember that no matter which method you use, your baby can and will learn to communicate using signs as long as you are consistent in your practice. As you continue to read about these methods, you will see that they each have pros and cons.

Although each technique has its benefits, this book focuses primarily on the use of American Sign Language (ASL) due to its uniformity and common usage among signing babies. All of the signs included in the back of the book and on the DVD are standard ASL signs. You will find, however, that the tips and information throughout this book will be helpful to you no matter which method you choose.

American Sign Language

If you have ever witnessed people speaking in sign in the United States or Canada, they were most likely using ASL. ASL is the most commonly used sign language and the fourth most common language overall in the United States. It is independent of English and offers a complete vocabulary and its very own syntax. It was developed by Deaf Americans to facilitate communication between one another. Although variations have been in use much longer, standardization of ASL began in 1817 when the first school for the Deaf was established in the United States.

E-ALERT

Although ASL is the most commonly used sign language in the United States, it is not the only one. There are other sign language dialects, such as Pidgin Signed English, that differ from ASL. If your goal is to use ASL, be sure that you only use study materials specifically labeled as such.

If you choose to use ASL signs with your baby, you will be using basic signs to enhance communication between your child and those around her. You will not be required to learn the grammatical rules of the language. As your child gets older, however, she may wish to become fluent in ASL. If so, it will be necessary for her to learn the grammatical rules and structure of the language. When that time comes, consider enrolling her in an ASL class. Better still, you might want to take a class together. You and your child will share many hours of quality time as you learn and practice this second language.

Why Choose American Sign Language?

Many parents choose ASL for their babies because they are inspired by the beauty of the language. If you have ever seen a parent and a baby signing together, you have witnessed this beauty for yourself. It provides a sweetly intimate way for parents to communicate with their babies. As an added bonus, the beautiful yet somewhat intricate ASL signs can improve a child's fine motor skills. Understand, of course, that a baby or young toddler will not be able to form every sign perfectly, particularly those that require a great deal of dexterity.

How would you like for your child to have a head start on a second language? A large number of parents choose ASL in order to provide a foundation for a second language later in life. Babies who are continually exposed to signs have an early grasp of sign language that will better enable them to become fluent as they get older.

E-FACT

It is estimated that between 500,000 and 2 million people in the United States alone use ASL regularly. If your baby continues to study ASL into her childhood, she will have plenty of people with whom she can communicate.

While there are many compelling reasons to choose ASL, perhaps the biggest is that it offers a designated set of signs to use. You can simply open up an ASL dictionary and find the sign for the word you want to use. Similarly, other adults in your baby's life can follow suit and all participate in your child's learning experience. The choice of such a well-established language eliminates the confusion that can ensue from using home signs or a combination of signs.

It is important to note, however, that in spite of the uniformity that ASL provides, many signs have variations. In one part of the country you may see something signed one way, while in another region you may see the same word signed in a different way. In the same way, older generations may sign something one way while younger generations sign it differently. Just be sure that the adults in your baby's life are all on the same page.

What's Not to Love?

As babies struggle to communicate, they begin to make gestures of their own. Most of the ASL signs that you use with your child are likely to be quite different from the ones she has created. There are many ASL signs that are symbolic of the concepts and actions they express, but even those may not mimic the signs your baby has created for herself. To that degree, it may be a struggle for your baby to begin using ASL signs over her own gestures. It is important to note, though, that the primary purpose of using baby sign language is to enable your baby to communicate. If she has certain words or ideas that she is able to express through her own signs, perhaps it is unnecessary to introduce alternative signs.

Home Signs and Baby Gestures

Home signs (also known as *baby gestures*) is another popular and well-accepted method of signing with babies. Simply put, home signs are typically parent-invented signs that resemble the word or action they symbolize. Here are a few ideas for home signs:

- BATH: Pretend to rub soap over your arms as if taking a bath.
- BOTTLE: Make a fist and bring the index finger end of it up to your lips as if putting a bottle in your mouth.
- CUP: Cup your hand as if holding a glass and raise it to your mouth. Note that this is also the ASL sign for DRINK.
- DIAPER: Simply pat the diaper area to indicate a change is needed.
- DOG (or CAT): Pretend you are petting a dog or cat from head to tail.
- SLEEP: For a familiar gesture, just tilt your head to one side, resting it on your open hand.

If you choose to use home signs, you will quickly figure out which signs work best for your child. She may find some easier than others, and you may have to adapt them to fit her needs. As you introduce your child to each new sign, be sure to document it for easy reference later. If you forget a sign, things can get very complicated for your baby.

The Benefits of Home Signs

One of the biggest benefits of home signs is that there is little to learn. You simply make up your own signs and, perhaps, also use the ones that your baby has created. Most of these self-made signs will reflect the words that they symbolize, as you can see from the examples above. Because home signs are generally iconic, they may be more akin to a baby's natural gestures.

> ### E-SSENTIAL
>
> Before you write off ASL in favor of home signs, keep in mind that quite a few ASL signs are remarkably iconic. As you browse through the signs included in this book, you may be surprised to see that many of them mimic a characteristic of the thing they represent.

Another argument for the use of home signs is that you can create signs that are easier for babies to form. Many ASL signs would be too difficult for a baby to use, but when you make up your own signs, you can keep your baby's limitations in mind. Using one-handed signs, single-motion signs, and signs that require less dexterity will all help your baby to master a sign sooner.

If you like the idea of home signs but do not want to make up a complete vocabulary, some programs of instruction include a standard set of baby-friendly gestures for all participants to use. These courses offer the benefit of iconic signs that are easy for baby to form and eliminate the need for you to come up with your own signs. You may want to try out different programs to find the best fit for you and your baby.

The Problem with Home Signs

The problem with home signs is that there is no universal set of signs. Even if you take a class, your baby will only be able to communicate with others who have taken that particular course of instruction. If you do not take a class or have a course book, then your baby's communication is limited further. Unless you constantly update family and caregivers with each new sign, other people will have a difficult time understanding your baby, thus defeating the purpose of using sign language to begin with.

In addition, home signs eliminate the early foundation for learning ASL later in your child's life. Your future goals for your child will determine if this is a factor for you at all. Of course, any child can be taught ASL, regardless of her background in sign. It is simply easier for the child who has already mastered many of the basic signs.

Baby-Modified American Sign Language

At some point (probably sooner rather than later), your baby is going to attempt a sign that you have taught her, but it will be altered due to her lack of dexterity or because she cannot quite grasp the exact formation. For instance, the ASL sign for EAT is to bring all five fingertips to the lips and tap twice (see Chapter 8). But your child might begin to tap her lips with one finger to tell you that she wants to eat. If you want, you can then adopt the one-finger-tap as your sign for EAT. This modified sign would then become part of your child's signing vocabulary.

E-ALERT

If you encourage your baby to use modified ASL signs, be aware that she could inadvertently modify a sign so that it takes on a different meaning entirely. This could cause confusion for her caregivers and anyone else with a basic understanding of ASL. Worse yet, she could turn a perfectly innocuous sign into something inappropriate.

It is worth noting that some babies tend to do more modifying than others. A sign that is particularly difficult for one child to master might be simple for another. As a result, your child's modified vocabulary might include one sign or ten or a hundred.

Why Encourage Baby to Modify Sign Language?

Baby-modified sign language offers more structure than home signs, as you still use a basic set of signs. At the same time, it provides more flexibility than true ASL, as signs can be adapted for ease of formation. The fact is that some signs are just more difficult than others, and some require a level of dexterity that a baby simply does not yet possess. By encouraging your baby to make modifications, you will reduce her level of frustration, which may come from being unable to form those toughest signs.

E-QUESTION

If my baby modifies some signs, will I be able to demonstrate the actual ASL signs later?

Yes. Without consistent reinforcement, babies will eventually stop using the signs they have been taught. After your child has gained verbal ability, simply drop the modified signs. When you are ready to increase your older child's signing vocabulary, begin adding in the correct ASL signs.

There may also be some times for you when it is helpful to do a little modifying of your own. A prime example is with the sign for DIAPER. To form this sign, you make pinching motions with both hands at your waist (as shown in Chapter 8). However, if you use a changing table to change your baby's diaper, the side of the table will likely obscure her view of your waist. You may then opt to make the same motion at a higher point on your body. Likewise, you may find that two-handed signs are difficult to demonstrate, as one of your hands is typically holding a baby. In that case, you might choose to change the sign by forming it with only one of your hands. If, however, you are finding it necessary to modify many signs, you might want to consider switching to home signs, in which you can create all of the signs yourself.

What's Wrong with Modified ASL?

With the benefits that come with modifying ASL signs to fit your needs, it seems like a good choice of methods. However, like the other methods that deviate from ASL, modified ASL can cause a few problems. Among a baby's peers who also use ASL, these altered signs may create a communication gap. Additionally, other people who sign with your baby (such as other family members and caregivers) will have to keep track of which signs have been modified and which have not.

> **E-FACT**
>
> Some baby-sign classes and groups use sets of signs that are based on a typical baby's natural gestures. As long as everyone in your signing circle uses the same set of signs, all of the babies and parents should be able to communicate with one another.

If you choose to continue to use sign language with your child as she gets older, these modified signs will be useless to her. It would be similar to teaching someone Spanish but making up gibberish to replace the occasional word. You might understand this language, but it would be meaningless in Mexico. Instead, you will have to go back and correct all of the signs that your baby has modified or that you have modified yourself. In the end, you may find that it would have been easier to reinforce the correct signs from the beginning.

A Combination of Methods

Some parents may choose to use a combination of methods. For example, perhaps you like the ASL sign for DRINK (cup your hand as if holding a glass and lift it to your mouth) but feel that the sign for EAT is too complicated. Perhaps you would rather make a motion like bringing a spoon to your mouth for this sign. If you choose to use a combination of methods, you could pick the signs you like best and either use modified ASL or home signs for the rest.

Many parents who combine methods primarily use ASL but change only the occasional sign. Unlike the changes made with modified ASL, these changed signs will usually bear no resemblance to the original sign. Instead, they are baby-friendly home signs that are symbolic of the word they represent. This is the lesser degree of combining methods and will be less confusing for you than combining to a greater degree.

E-ALERT

If you choose to use a combination of methods when signing with your baby, be sure to keep track of every sign for future reference. A photo album demonstrating each sign is a great way to document the signs you are using with your baby.

The Benefits of Combining Methods

Combining methods allows you to pick and choose the easiest signs for you and your baby. It offers the greatest flexibility by providing more structure and options than home signs and less rigidity than ASL. If, after reading about the various methods of sign-language instruction, you cannot decide on just one, or you want your child to reap the benefits of them all, then combining methods may be the best choice for you.

Why Not Combine Methods?

As with baby gestures and modified ASL, combining methods will render your baby at least partially "speechless" among other children who sign. If you belong to a signing playgroup or take a signing class, this will be of particular concern.

In addition, using a combination of techniques is going to create more work for you, as it is the most complicated method of instruction for you and the other signers in your baby's life. You, your family, and your baby's caregivers will all have to take note of every sign she learns. Some of her signs will be found in a standard ASL book, some will have been modified to fit her needs, while still others will be made up entirely. If you choose to go this route, you will want to devise a plan to keep all of your baby's signs well documented and organized.

Choosing the Right Method

There are many factors involved in choosing the right method for you and your baby. Each school of baby sign-language instruction comes with both advantages and problems. Each one has its own advocates. Likewise, each has its own critics. Try not to let this overwhelm you. Now that you have an understanding of the basic principles of each option, you are well equipped to choose the best one for you and your baby. If you are still unsure of the right method for you, here are a few things to consider:

- **Immediate goals:** Is your primary goal to give your baby a preverbal mode of communication?
- **Ease of use:** Is it important to you that sign language be a fun and easy activity for the whole family?
- **Simplicity of formations:** Do you prefer signs that are easy for you and your baby to sign and remember?
- **Communication with others:** Would you like your baby to be able to communicate with other signers her age?
- **Future goals:** Do you want your baby to have a head start on a second language?

The answers to these questions can help you determine the ideal method of instruction for you and your baby. Remember that there is no right way or wrong way to sign. Instead, there are just some methods that will fit your goals, lifestyle, and style of teaching better than others. Regardless of the method you choose, your child will be signing before you know it.

Chapter 4

Timing It Right

When should you begin signing with your baby? Is there ever a point at which you have missed your chance? The fact is that regardless of whether your baby was just born or is a walking and talking toddler, signing can still be beneficial to him. In this chapter, you will discover the optimal time for starting sign language and how long you can expect to wait for that first sign in return.

4

When Is the Right Time?

The general consensus among baby-signing experts is that six to eight months is the perfect age to begin introducing your baby to sign language. At around six months, a baby is gaining comprehension of language and probably understands a few words. At around seven months, babies have developed enough fine motor skills to form some basic signs. This physical and mental development is what makes sign language a valid form of communication for babies. In addition, most babies are alert, observant, and eager to learn during this age range.

It is important to note that regardless of the age at which you introduce sign language, it may be a few months before your baby signs back to you. Even babies who are introduced to sign language at six months most commonly make their first signs between eight and ten months of age.

Even though there are great benefits to introducing sign at this time, you can be just as successful if you begin earlier or later. If you have missed the six-to-eight-month range, start signing with your child now because it is never too late. Similarly, there is nothing wrong with demonstrating sign language to your four-, five-, or even one-month-old.

It's Never Too Early

If you are the parent of a newborn, you may be eager to get started. In the case of a baby under six months of age, "getting started" for a parent simply means learning and practicing the signs yourself. Although your baby may find your signing to be entertaining, he will not be able to sign back at this point, and he may not even pay attention. So why start early?

E-FACT

Many babies begin to respond to their names as early as four or five months of age, even though they may not understand any other spoken word. It is unknown if babies at this age actually understand that they are being addressed, or if they recognize the sound and pattern of their name because it is spoken so frequently.

There is one primary advantage to using sign language before a child is six months of age: It gets you into the practice of forming signs. If you make a habit of it early on, then signing will just come naturally to you. If you have decided you do not want to wait until your child is six months old before beginning to sign with him, here are a few tips to get you started:

- Don't get discouraged. Remember that because you are starting early, you will have to wait even longer to see that first sign.
- Focus on baby's earliest needs and interests. Choose signs that pertain to your young infant's everyday life. Good early signs include MILK, MOMMY, DADDY, and DIAPER.
- Be consistent. Don't change methods because you aren't seeing results. That will only set back your progress.
- Learn all you can. Because you will have a head start on your baby, it is a good time to learn the signs yourself.
- Don't pressure the skeptics. Because it will probably take months for your baby to begin signing, don't bother to push signing on the skeptics in your life until your baby is a little older or begins to sign.

It is important to understand that this early start will probably not make your baby any more proficient at sign language than his peers who begin at six months of age. Neither is your child likely to learn the signs any sooner. However, a parent who is in the habit of signing early on may be more consistent than a parent who is starting right along with her child. This, in turn, may mean that baby has an easier time learning to sign.

Better Late Than Never

So your child is ten months, eighteen months, or even twenty-nine months old, and you've just discovered the benefits of sign. Have you missed your chance? No! Your child can still benefit from sign. Understand, of course, that the extent of these benefits depends on his age and level of development. No matter how old or how advanced he is, however, there is never any harm in teaching your child a second language. In fact, children from birth to ten years of age can typically learn a second language almost as proficiently as their native language. So it is never too late to start!

Older Infants

Older infants usually have no trouble picking up signs. The biggest reason why it is better to introduce sign at six or seven months of age instead of eleven or twelve months is that by waiting, you miss out on some preverbal time in which your child could be signing. The other reason is that during the optimal age range, a baby is first starting to acquire language comprehension, which makes it an ideal time to begin learning a language.

> ## E-ALERT
>
> Don't be surprised if your older baby learns to say a word before he learns to sign it, particularly familiar words like "Mommy" or "bottle." This is because you will be speaking each word as you sign it, and an older baby has reached an age when he is likely trying to say his first words.

Keep in mind that a child who is nine, ten, or eleven months old is still in the early stages of language comprehension. Parents who begin using sign language during this stage usually find that their babies are quite successful. It seems that a briefly delayed start does not adversely affect a child's signing progress. The most important aspect of practicing sign language with a baby of any age is to sign frequently and consistently.

Toddlers and Beyond

The dynamics change a little as your child gets older. Once a toddler starts talking, he will be less motivated to sign. After all, he is able to ask for what he wants, so why bother signing? However, there are some words or concepts that may be too difficult for a young toddler to express verbally. In addition, toddlers and young children are better able to learn a second language than older kids. So if your child is a toddler or even a preschooler, he will still pick up the language better than an older child or adult.

When beginning sign language with a toddler or preschooler, consider starting with signs for words that your child has trouble pronouncing. As he probably gets frustrated when he is not understood, he will be motivated to use these signs. Of course, it is important to verbally say the word while demonstrating the sign to help him with his speech and to reiterate the meaning of the sign.

E-FACT

The average toddler has a vocabulary of 300 spoken words by the time he is two and a half years old. In addition, he will likely be able to understand approximately 900 words. By this point, he will also be constructing simple sentences of two or three words.

If your child resists using signs, even for the words he has trouble pronouncing, continue to demonstrate the signs in his presence. Eventually, he will probably start to sign, too. If, however, the stubborn nature of the terrible twos makes him especially resistant to signing, consider holding off until he is a few months older and a bit more agreeable.

Does Time of Day Matter?

While it is true that there are periods throughout a baby's day in which he is more alert, signing opportunities may not always occur during those periods. It is one thing to wait for such a time before reading a book to your child or doing an activity with him, but you don't necessarily have that option with signing. Signing opportunities crop up at all sorts of times throughout the day, including mealtimes, diaper changes, outside time, and numerous other times when your baby may or may not be at his most alert. All of this is not to say that you cannot take advantage of times when your baby is most alert. On the contrary, you should watch for these moments and use them to introduce a sign for a toy, a pet, or another interesting object.

There is at least one sign that cannot be taught during an alert period and that instead must be demonstrated at bedtime and naptime. That sign, of course, is SLEEP. Your child will not understand the concept of sleep unless he is sleepy or preparing to go to bed.

E-SSENTIAL

If you are trying to determine your child's periods of alertness, there are a few points throughout the day that are often a baby's best times for learning. While every baby is different, watch for alertness during the following times: after feedings but before naptimes, early evening before bed, and about an hour after waking up in the morning.

Your signing efforts will be most effective if you demonstrate the signs at a natural time. Signing, after all, must become a way of life for you and your baby. The best way for that to happen is to incorporate baby sign language as seamlessly as possible into everything you do.

Choosing the Right Environment

An environment free from distractions is certainly the best environment in which to learn anything, including sign language. On the other hand, an environment with a lot of stimulation provides many things that can be labeled with signs. The key to striking the right balance is to choose an environment that is free from unnecessary distractions such as the television blaring, another child running through the room, or the incessant ringing of the telephone. There are times when these distractions cannot be avoided, but when possible, keep them to a minimum.

Environments for Beginning Signers

When you first introduce signs to your child, any distraction can be problematic. At this point in your signing adventures, you are introducing your baby to more than just the signs themselves. You are demonstrating the concept of signing. He is learning that signing is a form of communication and that he can use it to express himself. If your baby has his mind on something else, he is less likely to pick up the sign or to make the connection between the sign and communication.

For example, imagine that you are feeding your baby a bottle before naptime. You know that he routinely falls asleep during this feeding, so you have gotten into the habit of turning on the television. Unbeknownst to you, however, your baby is watching or listening to the television, too. If that's the case, he is unlikely to get much out of your sign demonstrations. In addition, if you are engrossed in something else, you may even forget to sign for your baby.

For Advanced Signers

Babies and toddlers who have a firm grasp on the concept of sign language will begin to learn signs faster and more easily than they did in the beginning. At some point, it seems to click in their little minds that signing is a way to ask for what they want or to express their feelings or observations. When that happens, they are usually eager to sign, and you will not have to struggle for their attention. In fact, many babies at this stage will point to an object or ask, "What's that?" because they want you to label it with a sign.

E-FACT

An effective way to help encourage your child's language development and build his vocabulary is to verbally label everything around you. Household objects, outdoor sights, and people should all be labeled. Once you get into the habit of verbally labeling, it will be easy to then make the sign for the object in addition to speaking the verbal label.

By the time your baby reaches this stage, sign language will have become a routine part of his life and yours. Neither of you will have to think too hard about signing, and both of you will do it out of habit. Because you will not be planning out your signing times, but rather will be doing it all the time, it will be hard to avoid distraction. Instead, if your baby seems distracted while you are introducing a new sign, try to get his attention by calling his name or snapping your fingers. If he is not willing to focus, wait until another time to demonstrate the sign.

Delayed Gratification

No matter when you start signing with your baby, the reality is that it will take a while to see results. Some babies start signing in just a few short weeks. Others may take several months. So what would cause one baby to sign early and another to sign later? There are several factors to consider, including the age of the baby, the frequency and consistency of the signs he is exposed to, and even his temperament. A stubborn baby may resist signing, while a curious baby may be intrigued by it. A baby who loves to perform may be eager to sign, while a passive baby may be oblivious to your efforts. It all boils down to the fact that every baby is a unique individual and as such, each will develop various skills (including signing) at his own pace. While you do not have any control over your child's personality or stage of development, you can encourage his signing endeavors by being consistent and offering abundant praise.

E-ALERT

Although it is necessary to sign repeatedly to your child, be careful not to overload him with too many different signs in the beginning. This could result in confusion. Once he begins to sign on his own, feel free to add in as many signs as you want.

Just Keep Signing!

In the film *Finding Nemo*, one character, Dory, has a personal mantra of "Just keep swimming. . . ." This philosophy keeps her going strong, even when things aren't going as well as she might like. In the same way, "Just keep signing!" should be the signing parent's mantra. That persistence and determination is *the* key to using sign language with your baby.

As a signing parent, you will soon find that "Just keep signing" proves to be the answer to almost every signing dilemma. What should you do if your baby won't sign to you? Just keep signing! What if your baby isn't forming a sign correctly? Just keep signing! What should you do if your baby forgets a sign? Just keep signing! Sounds simple, doesn't it? That's because it is.

Why It Pays to Be Patient

At some point in your signing journey, you may experience doubt that your baby will ever learn to sign, frustration that your efforts seem to be fruitless, or impatience with your baby's slow progress. These are feelings that plague many signing parents because practicing sign language with a baby can be a thankless job with little reward—at least at first. If you *just keep signing*, however, your baby will begin to understand your signs. Shortly after that, your baby will finally sign to you.

E-SSENTIAL

While it is helpful to see that other babies have successfully learned to sign, remember that every baby is different and develops at his own pace. Just because it took one baby three months to form his first sign doesn't mean it will take your baby that long. Likewise, other babies may learn to sign before yours does.

If you feel discouraged, surround yourself with signing babies in a class or a playgroup. Seeing all of those signing success stories will motivate you to be patient and stick it out. Those other babies didn't learn to sign overnight. Instead, their parents spent many weeks repeating signs over and over again—just like you. If these parents have seen results, you can be sure that you will, too.

For all of your efforts, there is no greater reward than to see your baby sign. That very first sign validates the weeks and months put into this endeavor and it is a unique milestone for which you and your baby should be proud. From here, your baby will seem to pick up one new sign after another, making all of your patience and determination worthwhile.

Chapter 5

Getting Everyone Involved

The more people you can get actively involved in signing with your baby, the easier the task will be. A child who is surrounded by sign will learn it much more quickly than a child who only has one person instructing her. In this chapter, you will learn about getting others involved in baby sign language and discover how to overcome skepticism from loved ones and criticism from strangers.

5

Understanding Skepticism

When you first announce to your spouse, your parents, or your friends that you are going to be using sign language with your baby, don't be surprised if you are met with less-than-favorable reactions. You may have some loved ones who find the very idea of sign language for babies odd, while others may actually disapprove.

One argument that signing parents encounter is that sign language for babies is just a fad. Because it is a more recent practice and because it is growing in popularity, some people may see it as a passing trend. If you want, you can delve into baby sign language's proven benefits with these people who call it a fad, but you might find it easier to respond with something such as this: "If it is going to help my baby communicate with me, who cares if it's a fad?"

E-FACT

Baby sign language is hardly an emerging trend. It has actually been practiced for more than twenty years. In fact, the most prominent research on the subject of signing with babies took place in the mid-1980s. Of course, since the beginning of time, babies have likely been gesturing to get their needs met.

Another form of skepticism you may encounter is the belief that babies can't actually learn to sign. People who believe this will probably not be open to evidence that proves them wrong. Therefore, your best strategy is to let your baby prove it to them. It is just a matter of time before your baby is signing. That should make a believer out of anyone.

Finally, you may find that your loved ones are concerned that you are trying to turn your child into a super-baby. They may fear that you are forcing sign language on your little one and not allowing her to be a child. This is an understandable concern from people who are not familiar with the practice of baby sign language. Try to explain to them that gesturing is a natural part of a baby's communication development, and then show them how easily you incorporate signing "lessons" into your child's regular routine. This will usually alleviate this type of concern.

Involving Both Parents

As with many other aspects of parenting, it is common for one parent to support the idea of baby sign language and the other to dismiss it. If you find yourself wanting to use sign language with your child, but your partner isn't enthusiastic, this section is for you.

If you want to convince your parenting partner that baby sign language is a worthwhile undertaking, you will first have to determine what objections you are facing. Does your baby's other parent think it is a waste of time? Does she think it will require too much effort? Could it be that she doubts its effectiveness? When you know why your partner is resistant, you will be better equipped to change her mind.

Even the most skeptical parent may be swayed to participate when he realizes that signing is an opportunity for the family to do something collectively. Gather the family together to practice signs or to watch a signing video; have a "secret" conversation with your partner or kids while out in public; compare notes with your partner at the end of the day about your baby's signing progress. By making it a family affair, your baby's other parent might be more willing to give it a try.

E-ALERT

Don't let your newfound passion for baby sign language cause strife within your home. Your baby can and will learn sign language, even if you are the only one signing with her. If you are unable to get your partner on board, just do it yourself. Your baby will still benefit, and your partner may eventually change his mind.

Even if your partner is not resistant to the idea of signing, he may still not take an active role in it. He may feel that he is inadequate to sign with your baby, or he may not think it is worth the effort. In either case, you can try to draw him in and get him involved. For example, if he does not take it upon himself to pick up a sign language book and read it or to learn the signs some other way, you will have to guide him in signing. Each time you learn a new sign, show it to your parenting partner as well. Give him opportunities to sign to your baby, and encourage him to actively seek those opportunities himself.

It is possible that your child's other parent may still choose not to participate even after all of your encouragement, whether because she is uninterested or because she is still skeptical. In that case, wait until your baby forms her first sign. The thrill of that impressive milestone may be just the motivation your parenting partner needs to get on board.

Caregiver Participation

Ideally, babysitters, day-care teachers, and other caregivers will learn to sign right alongside you and your baby. Unfortunately, however, these are often the hardest people to get involved. Babysitters, particularly those who only sit for you occasionally, will be reluctant to invest their time in learning to sign. Day-care teachers may like the idea, but they may have too many other children in their care to devote much time to learning how to communicate one-on-one with your baby. In spite of these hurdles, it is worth trying to get these people involved if you can. After all, these caregivers may spend a great deal of time with your baby and could greatly influence her signing progress.

Babysitters

A Saturday-night sitter may or may not see the importance of learning to sign with your baby. If she does not and absolutely refuses to have any part of it, all is not lost. Someone who sits for a couple of hours now and then is not going to make or break your signing efforts. That being said, it is helpful to get anyone on board who is willing, so it is still worth it to give it a try.

For the reluctant babysitter, make it easy by providing a signing reference sheet. Go over your baby's most commonly used signs as well as any variations that she makes to them. You could also offer to loan your sitter a book so that she can read about the practice in her spare time. If you have older children who are practicing sign language with your baby, their influence might encourage your sitter to participate.

If you are lucky enough to have a babysitter who is receptive to the idea of sign, offer her the materials she needs to learn your baby's signs. This could include books, videos, Web sites, or anything else that demonstrates the signs your baby has learned. Then, because a signing sitter is such a rare commodity, recommend her to the other parents in your signing circle, and be sure to let your sitter know that you are doing so.

Day-Care Teachers

Because they may have seen baby sign language used before, experienced day-care workers may be more open to it than some people you encounter. Day-care workers also typically have training in child development and may understand the benefits that sign language provides. Even if your day-care provider is supportive of baby sign language, however, she may not be eager to participate. After all, she is likely quite busy with several infants in her care and may not feel like she has time to take on signing with your baby.

E-FACT

The National Association for the Education of Young Children recommends that child-care centers maintain a ratio of one teacher to no more than four infants. Some day-care centers opt for a ratio of one to three. Even if she is only caring for three babies, a teacher undoubtedly has her hands full for most of the day.

If your baby's teacher is resistant, try making it as easy for her as possible. Ask her if she would consider learning your child's top three (or five or ten) signs. You could also share with her all of the benefits that baby sign language has to offer and then suggest that she use it with the entire class. Even if she is unwilling to sign *with* your baby, provide her with a reference sheet so that she can understand your baby when he signs to her.

This is not to say that all day-care teachers will be reluctant to practice sign with your child. On the contrary, some will be happy to help, or you may find that your child's caregiver is already familiar with some of the basic signs. Some day cares may even use sign language as part of their curriculum.

Whether you are able to get your child's day care on board or not, it never hurts to ask. If the caregiver won't participate, you are out nothing. If she will, however, your baby will benefit tremendously by having another prominent person in her life signing with her.

Teaching Family Members

Once you have convinced your family that baby sign language is worthwhile, it is time to show them the basics. It is not necessary for every member of your family to become fluent in sign language. Instead, have them focus only on the signs your baby is learning. This will make the process less daunting for them.

The first people you want to learn the signs are your baby's siblings. Most babies are fascinated by their older siblings and love to watch their every move. Additionally, because your other children probably live in the same house as your baby, they are everyday role models for sign. Demonstrating sign language to your older kids is a simple process, as you can show signs to them at the same time you are signing with your baby. They will probably think it's cool and will pick up most of the basic signs very quickly. If it sparks an interest in them, consider enrolling them in an American Sign Language class so that they may learn the language beyond its basics. Most kids enjoy learning sign language and will have fun using it amongst themselves. Just keep in mind that if they become fluent, they will be able to carry on secret conversations to which you will not be privy!

Beyond the members of your household, you will also want to show members of your extended family the basic signs. If you have relatives who are interested in baby sign and eager to learn, give them a book or a DVD.

You can tell them which signs you plan to use and keep them updated as you introduce new signs to your baby. If you have loved ones who are reluctant or hesitant to sign, you may need to guide them through the process by showing them each sign as you use it with your baby. Try to make the process as simple as possible for all parties involved, and remind them that signing with a baby should be simple and fun.

E-SSENTIAL

For a fun way to get the whole family involved, consider throwing a signing party. Hire a sign language instructor to come to your home for an hour and show everyone the basics. Invite all your loved ones and serve a little finger food for an instant party.

Perhaps the most challenging family members to get on board are those who live out of town. You (and they) may think that it is unnecessary for them to participate in signing, but if they visit frequently, or if your baby visits them, it is just as important for them to learn the signs as well. As with other family members, you could simply send them a book or DVD and tell them which signs your baby is learning. For a creative twist, record your baby while she forms the signs. Then send the recording via mail or e-mail to your relatives. They will delight in watching the footage of your baby, and they will also get a signing lesson.

Handling Criticism from Strangers

If you ever sign with your baby in public, you are likely to get a lot of stares and probably a few comments. As peculiar as it may seem, many people appear to feel that they have an obligation to offer you unsolicited advice when it comes to signing with your child. It is common for signing parents to find that they encounter quite a bit of criticism from perfect strangers.

Most of the criticism is based on the myths you already read about in Chapter 1. People who buy into these myths are simply uneducated about sign language for babies. If you feel so inclined, use criticism from strangers as an opportunity to share with others the tremendous benefits that baby sign language can provide. You might even influence another parent to sign with her baby.

E-QUESTION

How can I tell strangers to mind their own business?

By doing just that. A polite but effective way to tell people to butt out is to respond like so: "Thank you, but I think I have it all under control." It isn't rude, but it conveys the clear message that you are not interested in unsolicited advice.

Although you may rationally understand that it does not matter what anyone thinks of your parenting methods, it is worth noting that criticism—even from a perfect stranger—can leave you wondering if the criticism is founded. You may find yourself questioning your motives and methods. You may begin wondering if your baby is truly benefiting from your efforts. If this happens, try to refocus on the positive aspects of signing, and look at the rewards that it brings. Most importantly, remember that you are giving your child a gift that will last a lifetime.

Dealing with Questions

Sometimes, it will be questions that you are besieged with instead of comments. These questions might seem critical in nature, or they may simply stem from honest curiosity. Whether you answer them is entirely up to you. However, remember that you have the opportunity to educate people each time you talk to them about baby sign language. Here are some common questions you may encounter and possible responses for them.

Questions from the Curious

"Is that sign language?"

The easiest answer to this question is a simple yes. However, you might want to offer a brief explanation as to why you and your baby are signing. You might say something like this:

"Yes, it is. I'm signing to help her communicate until she learns to talk. It has been a lot of fun for both of us."

You may also get a lot of questions from children who wonder what you are doing. A simple explanation will usually suffice, but be prepared to be inundated with numerous follow-up questions, as children are often insatiably curious.

Personal Questions

"Is your baby deaf?" or *"Are you deaf?"*

If you are speaking each word as you sign it, most people (though not all) will assume that it is your baby, and not you, who is deaf. Many people will not be so bold as to ask about your child's hearing ability, but occasionally, you will encounter a stranger who is. Here is a suggested response to this question:

"No. My daughter and I use sign language while she is learning to speak. It allows us to talk to each other while her speech is still developing."

How-To Questions

"How did you show your baby how to use sign language?"

Unless you have a lot of time to chat with the asker of this question, you will want to find some way to sum up the process in just a couple of sentences. Often, the person who asks this question is interested in signing with her own baby. If that seems to be the case, it is a good idea to recommend a book, DVD, or class to the prospective signer. Here is one way to address the question:

"It is really simple, but it takes time and patience. I just had to introduce one sign at a time and practice it over and over with my baby. If you are interested in learning more about it, you might want to check out (insert book title, DVD title, or class name here)."

The Speech-Delay Myth Revisited

"Will your baby ever learn to talk?"

As you read in Chapter 1, the myth of speech delays in signing babies is a common one. Because it is so widespread, you will likely encounter this misconception in the form of both questions and criticisms.

E-FACT

There is an analogy commonly used in signing circles that compares crawling to signing. This analogy states that in the same way that crawling strengthens leg muscles and helps a baby learn to walk, signing improves language development and helps a baby learn to talk.

Obviously, you will probably not want to quote entire research studies on the subject, but a brief answer such as this one will likely satisfy both the curious and the pushy:

"It has actually been proven that babies who learn sign language may develop more advanced speech skills than other babies. Not only that, but signing babies often have higher IQ scores later in life."

Chapter 6

Immerse Yourself in Sign

The best way to make signing a natural part of your life is to expose yourself to it on a regular basis. In this chapter, you will discover materials and resources to help you do just that. You will find that the more you immerse yourself in sign language, the better a signer you will be in your own right, and the more capable you will be as a model for your child.

The Buddy System

Do you have a friend with a baby around the same age as yours? Then why not sign together? There are so many advantages to signing with a friend. Not only will you have someone to share your excitement and your frustration, your baby will have a signing buddy, and you and your friend can swap tips on best and worst practices. Even if you have a friend who does not sign with her baby, use your own expertise to show her how fun, easy, and rewarding it can be. You may influence her to begin signing, resulting in a signing buddy for you.

E-ALERT

Do not compare your baby's signing progress with any other baby's. If another child begins to sign before your child does, it doesn't mean that your child is any less smart or capable. It simply shows that each baby progresses at his own rate.

Try to find a signing partner who uses the same method as you, whether that method is ASL, baby gestures, or some combination of the two. This will ensure that the two of you are using similar, if not the same, signs. Consider getting together for a weekly sign-and-play date. Not only will you and your baby have someone to sign with, but the children will have fun and you can enjoy adult conversation with your friend.

If you do not have a signing friend, consider "buddying up" with your child's other parent or another close family member. The two of you can practice signing with one another, and both of you can help your child learn to sign. The more people in your household who sign, the easier it will be for you and your baby.

Baby-Sign Classes

There are countless baby-sign classes all over the country. These classes use every method imaginable to teach sign. Some focus on American Sign

Language. Others use baby gestures. If you are unsure of which method you want to use, find several programs in your area and ask if you can attend a free introductory class for each one. Check out a couple of different methods, and see which one feels right for you and your child.

E-FACT

Many baby-sign programs will allow you to browse through their class materials without actually having to sign up for the class. This will allow you to get a feel for the class, the method it uses, and possibly even background information on the program or instructor.

Is it necessary to take a baby sign-language class? No. All that is required to introduce sign language to your baby is a small amount of signing know-how and a lot of patience and determination. You can acquire the signing know-how from many sources: a book, DVD, a class, or from another signer. The patience and determination are things that come with time. That said, however, a class can certainly enhance the signing experience. It will also introduce you to other signing parents and your child to other signing babies.

Baby-Sign Playgroups

Because baby sign is becoming so prevalent, you can find entire playgroups of signers. A signing playgroup will get together on a regular basis, usually weekly, in a home or a public location. Each group is different: You may find that some focus more on playing while others place more emphasis on signing. You may also discover that some groups of signers use ASL, while others use home signs or baby gestures. The groups that use baby gestures may not all be using the same signs, so the babies are not able to communicate with each other as effectively. Nonetheless, you can still find support and socialization within these groups.

Where to Find One

If signing playgroups seem to be elusive, you will be surprised at how very easy they can be to find and how many there actually are. A great place to start your search is with baby sign-language instructors. Ask around, and see if they know of any signing playgroups. Even if they don't, some of their clients might. Another resource is national playgroup databases that can easily be found online, such as Playgroups USA (*www.playgroupsusa.com*) or My Playgroups (*www.myplaygroups.com*). These databases will allow you to search for playgroups based on criteria such as location and focus of the group.

E-SSENTIAL

Playgroups, whether signing-focused or not, provide your child the opportunity to socialize with his peers. Equally important, playgroups give *you* the opportunity to socialize with other parents. No matter what type of playgroup you prefer, try to make this a regular part of you and your baby's schedule.

In spite of these databases and the many other resources available to you, it is still possible that you won't be able to find a playgroup to fit your needs. The good news is that some of these same databases will allow you to register your own playgroup. The following section describes how to start a signing group of your own.

How to Start a Baby-Sign Playgroup

If you can't find a signing playgroup in your area, why not start one? Playgroups are easy to organize and do not require a huge investment in time, as they can be as structured or as casual as you want them to be. Best of all, you can tailor the playgroup to fit your needs. For instance, do you need a group that meets on the weekends? What about a group geared toward one-year-olds exclusively? How about a group of single dads? If you form your own group, you can design it any way you want.

When you decide to organize your own group, the first thing you want to do to is to select the location for your get-togethers. If the prospective members of your group are people you do not know, start with a public place like a park or a playground. If your group members consist of friends, friends of friends, or relatives, you could meet in a different home each time.

Next, plan a time for your group to meet. How frequently do you want the group to get together? Will the group be accessible to working parents and meet on weekends or evenings, or do you want to meet during the day? Be sure to consider typical nap- and mealtimes, and try to work around them. After all, you don't want a herd of hungry or sleepy toddlers on your hands!

E-FACT

The average toddler needs twelve to thirteen hours of sleep per day. While they get a great deal of that sleep at night, until they are three or four years of age, most children also take an afternoon nap. The length of that nap varies from one child to another, but one to two hours is typical.

Once these details are in place, you can begin to recruit members for your group. The obvious place to start is within your own circle of friends. Do you know other signing parents who might be interested? Let them know about your group. Also let local baby sign-language instructors know so that they can pass along the information to their clients. Finally, register your group with an online database so that other parents can find you with the click of a mouse.

Other Materials That Demonstrate Signs

There are many books and DVDs or videos that show you how to sign with your baby. Other materials, however, can also enhance your signing experi- ence. While these extra materials are by no means necessary for successful signing, they can certainly help. After all, any added exposure to sign language is of benefit to you and your signing baby. Keep in mind also that while one parent may find these materials to be invaluable, another may find that her baby is uninterested in them. If the extra learning materials you try do not impress either you or your baby, don't feel that it is necessary to continue pushing them.

Flash Cards

A typical deck of baby sign-language flash cards depicts an object or concept on one side of each card and the corresponding sign on the other. These cards work just like any other kind of flash card. The idea is that you show your baby the picture side and give him the opportunity to form the sign.

These cards are best used for reinforcing the signs you have already taught your child. If possible, it is better to use a real-life object to first introduce a sign. This will give your baby a deeper understanding of the sign and make it more memorable for him. You could also use the flash cards to illustrate signs for objects that your baby does not normally encounter in his everyday life, such as exotic animals or out-of-the-ordinary places.

Storybooks

Signing storybooks are ideal for babies and toddlers. These books generally present a story interspersed with signing opportunities. Some may contain illustrations of signs, and some may have photographs. As with flash cards, these books are ideal for reiterating the signs your child already knows. Furthermore, he will probably be excited at the opportunity to sign along with the story. Don't be surprised, however, if your baby is too eager to turn the pages to bother with signing. As he gets a little older, he will be more likely to sit still and take in the story. See Appendix A for some suggested sign-language storybooks that you can find at your local library or bookstore.

The Deaf Community

Perhaps the best way to immerse yourself in sign is by getting involved with the Deaf community. The Deaf community is comprised of people who are physically deaf and hard of hearing, as well as those who subscribe to the Deaf culture or way of life, regardless of whether they have hearing loss.

E-ALERT

Do not assume automatically that an individual who is communicating in sign language is deaf. Many other people use this language, too, including those who have mild to moderate hearing loss, those with speech impairments, and those who have friends or loved ones who use sign.

All of these individuals in the Deaf community have one thing in common: They all use means of communication other than the spoken word. Spending time with them is a good way to see how people interact when sign language is their native "tongue." Not only will you gain insight into signing, but you will also have the opportunity to witness this beautiful language in action.

Deaf Culture

Many people who are deaf or hard of hearing do not consider themselves as having a disability. On the contrary, they embrace who they are and proudly consider themselves to be part of Deaf culture. The cultural Deaf are linked primarily by their use of American Sign Language. They also share common values, backgrounds, and lifestyles. The vast majority of the culturally Deaf have no desire to be assimilated into the hearing world.

Because of this tremendous pride, many culturally Deaf people are more than willing to teach others about their culture and their language. In fact, many Deaf community centers, churches, and clubs are open to everyone, with the idea of teaching the hearing community about Deaf culture. Always be open about your reasons for being present, and make it clear that you respect and admire their language. You will probably find that many people are happy to share their expertise with you.

Deafness as a Physical Condition

There are some individuals who are deaf or hard of hearing who are not culturally Deaf. They may not use American Sign Language, or they may prefer to be as much a part of the majority culture as possible. People who are deaf, but are not culturally Deaf, can also provide much insight into sign language, even if they do not use ASL.

> **E-SSENTIAL**
>
> Hearing-impaired individuals who do not use American Sign Language use other methods to express themselves, including reading lips, using another form of sign language, or using natural gestures. Often, you will find that such gestures are very similar to the natural gestures a baby uses.

Many of these individuals use gestures or other nonverbal ways of communicating. Pay attention to the way they interact with each other, and note any creative gestures they use. You might learn a few things that will help you and your baby with your own signing endeavors.

Sharing Your Knowledge with Others

As you become more and more familiar with baby sign language, you will have opportunities to share your knowledge with others. People will begin to ask you about your signing experiences, and many will want recommendations for materials or methods. If you are the only signing parent in your child's playgroup or day-care class, you may be asked to consider demonstrating baby sign language to the rest of the parents and children.

Likewise, some signing parents are making a business out of signing. They are holding baby-sign classes in homes, community centers, and churches. Some signing parents are affiliated with a baby sign-language program, and some work independently. If you decide to teach baby sign in any capacity, there are some things to keep in mind.

Certification and Training

Do you need special training or certification to teach baby sign language? Yes and no. You certainly want to be familiar enough with the practice of baby sign language if you are going to share your knowledge with others. For this reason, it is a good idea to take a class on the subject. This not only gives you additional training, it also gives you the opportunity to watch another teacher in action.

E-FACT

Colleges all over the nation offer courses in American Sign Language. The courses can be taken as part of a degree program or individually for continuing education credits. While these classes generally do not focus on sign language for babies, they will give you a solid introduction to the language.

As for certification, there are companies out there that will "certify" you to teach baby sign. All you have to do is pay a fee, and they will send you teaching materials. While the materials themselves may be helpful if you are teaching a group of parents and babies, the certification is often meaningless. This is not to say that there aren't legitimate programs out there. On the contrary, there are excellent programs available that will actually train you to be a baby sign-language instructor. Just remember that any certification you are given simply for paying a fee probably isn't worth much.

Understanding Your Students

Whether you are teaching sign language to the babies in your playgroup or are considering teaching baby sign language as your new part-time job, one element will remain the same: your clients. As a baby sign-language instructor, whether for fun or profit, your students will all be babies and toddlers. Because it has probably been quite a while since your own toddlerhood, it is a good idea to learn a thing or two about these small creatures.

Having a baby of your own is great practice, of course, but all babies are different. To develop a greater understanding of babies, toddlers, and how they communicate, consider taking a course in early childhood development, or pick up some books on the subject. Learn about typical growth and development of babies and toddlers, and try to gain some insight into their behavior patterns. The better you understand your students, the more likely they are to understand your signs.

Chapter 7

Getting Started

You have chosen the right signing method for you and your baby. You have waited for just the right phase in your baby's development, and you have even managed to get everyone on board. It's time to get started signing with your baby. The information in this chapter will provide you with advice to get you going, pitfalls to watch out for, and encouragement to keep you motivated. So get to it and happy signing!

Choosing Your Starter Words

Your baby's first experiences with sign will lay the foundation for all of her future signing endeavors. By carefully choosing fun and simple starter signs, you will provide her with a pleasurable signing experience that will motivate her to sign further. Some parents choose to start out with one or two signs, while others introduce four or five all at once. It is best to stay in the range of one to five signs to avoid overloading your baby with too much information too soon. Also remember that you will have to learn just as many signs as your baby, and you do not want to overload yourself, either.

> ## E-FACT
>
> Several American Sign Language signs incorporate a letter from the manual alphabet in their formation. For example, the sign for AUNT starts out with the letter A. For this reason, you may want to familiarize yourself with the ASL manual alphabet (see Appendix C) during the early stages of signing.

It is important to choose words that your baby will have an interest in signing. Initially, this interest will keep her riveted while you demonstrate the signs. As she begins to understand what the signs represent, it will be her interest that prompts her to imitate the signs. When she sees that signing brings a response, she will eagerly form the signs again and again.

In Chapter 8, you will find an extensive list of appropriate starter signs. Many of these signs fall into two different categories: high-impact signs and need-based signs. While you can certainly use any signs you wish, starting out with need-based or high-impact signs has its merits.

Need-Based Signs

An infant's needs are pretty basic. In fact, other than a whole lot of love, your baby probably requires little more than milk, clean diapers, and sleep. While that may seem simple enough, deciphering her cries can be quite a challenge. If only she could tell you exactly what she wants. By introducing need-based signs to your baby, you will be providing her with a vocabulary that will allow her to ask for the things that are most important to her. Examples of need-based signs include the following:

- DIAPER
- DRINK
- EAT
- MILK
- SLEEP

Need-based signs represent things that your baby is already very familiar with and things that she desperately wants to communicate. As she begins to comprehend that signing will enable her to communicate, she will eagerly attempt to form these signs.

High-Impact Signs

With their own unique personalities, all babies are fascinated and stimulated by different things. Perhaps your baby is excited by the family cat. Perhaps she is overjoyed by the sight of her blanket. Using the signs for things that interest your baby is a great way to motivate her as she begins her signing journey.

E-ALERT

Most babies have relatively short attention spans. The things that excite them this week may be perfectly mundane by the next. Be cautious when choosing high-impact signs, and try to stick to the ones that seem to have more staying power so that your baby doesn't lose interest in the sign.

Choosing high-impact signs for your baby's starter words is also a good way to encourage her exploration of the topics that interest her. If your baby is particularly excited by horses, for instance, then introducing the sign for HORSE is a good way to expose her not only to the word, but to examples of it. As you model the sign, you will likely be showing her actual horses, photos of horses, toy horses, and more. Because of her curiosity about the subject, she may quickly pick up the sign and learn more about horses as well.

A Note about Names

For some babies, it is not an object or a need that stimulates them most. For some babies, it is a special person in their lives who seems to excite them more than anything else. If that describes your baby, you may want to consider using a person as your starter sign.

Most of the people in your baby's life probably have a family title (Mommy, Daddy, Grandma, and so on) by which your baby knows them best. There are some people, however, whom your baby may know by an actual name (perhaps a sibling or a cousin). It is natural to want to incorporate signs for these people into your child's early signing vocabulary. However, it is important to note that names are generally spelled out in American Sign Language. (An illustration of the ASL manual alphabet can be found in Appendix C.) For a baby just learning to sign, however, trying to spell out a name would be a daunting, if not impossible, task. This is where creativity and flexibility will really come in handy. Here are some suggestions for dealing with names:

- Sign the person's title instead of their name. For example, your baby's cousin would simply be referred to using the sign for COUSIN.
- Sign the person's first initial, assuming there aren't too many people with the same initial in your baby's social circle.
- Fingerspell short names such as Joe or Ty.
- Make up a sign to represent each individual person. For example, if Aunt Lisa has long hair, then you might make a sign to indicate her hair.

In the end, you may decide that it is better to choose other starter words and hold off on names until your child is a little older and has more signing experience under her belt. If you do choose to demonstrate names to your baby, the way you ultimately handle it is up to you. When you find a method that works for you and your baby, stick with it.

E-SSENTIAL

There is no need to show your baby how to sign her own name—at least not right away. By the time your baby is old enough to sign, she will most certainly recognize her own name if she hears it spoken, and she will not have any real need to sign it herself. An older toddler or preschooler, however, will have fun learning how to spell her name in sign.

Introducing the Signs

Even after you have chosen the type of sign you are going to start with, you will still have to choose that very first sign. This may seem daunting, but there are really only two "rules" to keep in mind: Choose a sign that is easy for baby to form and one that you will have many opportunities to demonstrate.

For example, perhaps you have chosen MILK as the first sign you are going to introduce to your baby. This is a great first sign because it is easy to form and it can be used over and over every day. Introducing it is very easy. After your baby gets settled into your arms and begins to nurse or take a bottle, demonstrate the sign for MILK in her line of vision. Make the sign two or three times while also orally speaking the word each time. It is not necessary to repeat the motion throughout the entire feeding (your hand would surely grow weary). It is most important to demonstrate the sign at the beginning of the feeding. If she is not overtired or distracted by something else, she will likely watch your hand movement intently. If your baby looks away during the feeding and then looks back at you, you can certainly take the opportunity to demonstrate the sign again.

The key to signing with your baby is repetition. Every single time you feed her, you should form the sign for MILK. Likewise, if someone else feeds her, that person should demonstrate it as well. Another learning opportunity for your baby is while another child is drinking from a bottle or nursing. If you see that your baby notices the other child, speak the word "milk" out loud and then form the sign. The more often your baby is exposed to it and the more diligent you are, the faster she will learn the sign.

E-ALERT

Sometimes it may seem as if your baby just won't pay attention to a sign. Babies are easily distracted and will frequently look away. Since your baby will not acquire a sign the first time (or even the tenth time) you model it for her, don't worry if she looks away sometimes. Keep repeating the sign and she will eventually pick up on it.

Now that you have introduced your baby's first signs, you are going to be eagerly waiting for her to sign back. Unfortunately, this stage of the game requires a lot of patience on your part. Depending on when you begin using sign language with your baby, you may have weeks or months to wait before you see results. This delay can result in frustration for you and increased skepticism from others. If you feel yourself growing discouraged, just remember that babies everywhere are learning to sign. Your baby can, too. Don't give up. When your baby finally does sign back to you, it will have been worth the wait.

Take It Slow

Eventually, the magical day will come when your baby makes her first sign. It may be unsteady, but she will do it. You, of course, will be thrilled. Finally seeing results after weeks of waiting can give you a renewed sense of purpose. Now that you know your baby can and will sign, you may be tempted to demonstrate signs for everything you can think of. But doing this could hurt your child's progress instead of helping it. Too many signs at once (especially in the beginning) can result in your child getting her signs confused, feeling overwhelmed, or not comprehending the meanings of the signs.

Like any new skill, your baby will learn sign language one step at a time. It is best to introduce her to one or two signs, and when she has mastered those to introduce her to a couple more. Just don't forget to keep using the old signs after the new ones have been introduced. It is worth noting that after she has acquired the first few signs, the rest will probably come more quickly and easily. This is because your baby now comprehends the fact that signing is a way for her to communicate.

> **E-FACT**
>
> As slowly as signing may seem to come to your baby, it is a skill that can be acquired much earlier than speaking. While the average twelve-month-old may only have one to ten words in her spoken vocabulary, a signing baby can have two, three, or four times that many.

If your baby begins to show indications of confusion after using several signs, it may be time to slow down your signing. Do not add any more signs for a while, and continue to use the ones you have already been using with her. When she seems to have them down without any confusion, it will then be appropriate to introduce new signs again.

You may also notice that your baby seems to drop a sign now and then. One day she will be using a particular sign, and then suddenly it seems to be gone from her repertoire. Generally, this is because your baby is so busy demonstrating new signs that she can't be bothered with the old ones. Continue to model the sign in front of her, even when she isn't using it herself. This will help her to retain its meaning until she is ready to use it again.

Positive Reinforcement

As with everything your baby does, she will be looking to you to gauge your reaction when she begins to sign. Your response can make all the difference to her signing progress. When you react to your baby's accomplishment with excitement and pride, she is likely to want to repeat it.

When your baby learns a new sign, you may not recognize it at first. Therefore, be on the lookout for any gesture that at all resembles a sign you have been using with her. If you suspect she might have signed, react! It is better to react to nothing than to miss a chance at acknowledging her accomplishment.

E-FACT

Positive reinforcement works because children want the approval of their parents. Giving your child a lot of praise for a job well done also helps to instill in her a sense of pride. This pride in her own efforts and approval from you will encourage her to continue to sign.

Most importantly, never demand perfection from your child's signs or force her to sign in order to get what she wants. This will only frustrate her and cause her to want to give up. With patience and encouragement, your child *will* learn to sign.

Pile on the Praise

Praising your child for making a sign will probably come naturally to you. In fact, the first few times she signs, you will probably have a hard time containing your glee. Some great ways to praise your baby include clapping, telling her what a great job she did, offering a big smile or laugh, or hugging her. She will take great pride in herself when she sees that you are getting excited about something she has done. This praise will encourage her to sign over and over again. It is also a good idea to involve others in the praise. If both Mommy and Daddy are in the room, then they should both praise baby for a job well done.

Reactions Speak Louder Than Words

As important as praise is, the way you respond to your child's sign is even more important. Because every sign represents a word or an action, the best way to reinforce that comprehension is by reacting appropriately every time your child signs. When she forms the sign for EAT, feed her. When she makes the sign for DIAPER, change her. If you respond to her request quickly, she will soon learn that sign language is an effective way to get what she needs.

There may be times when you are unable to respond immediately to your baby's sign. For instance, if you are in the car in busy traffic and she makes the sign for DIAPER, you may be unable to change her right away. In a situation like that, acknowledge her request: "Oh, do you need a diaper?" Then assure her that you will change her as soon as you can stop. This will not be as effective as immediately giving her what she wants, but it will let her know that you understand and that you are acknowledging what she has said.

E-SSENTIAL

During this early stage of signing, it is particularly important that everyone who plays a role in your baby's daily life is familiar with the signs you are using and that they know how to react appropriately if your baby should sign. You wouldn't want your baby's first sign to go unnoticed because an unknowing caregiver missed it.

Your baby will soon discover that she can get what she wants—simply by signing. This dawning will be the start of her signing adventures. With this knowledge, your baby will want to learn as many signs as she can.

Speak Up!

Although sign language is a wonderful form of communication, your baby will still someday need to learn to talk. Sign language can actually improve her language acquisition skills if you simply incorporate the spoken word with the signing one. Each time you form a sign, label it with the corresponding spoken word. Likewise, if your baby forms a sign, reiterate the spoken word as you address her request.

In addition to simply labeling the word, it is also beneficial to a baby's vocabulary and understanding of the English language to use the word in context. For example, if you are demonstrating the sign for BLANKET, you might say something like this:

"Blanket. Let's cover you up with your blanket."

Or if your baby makes the sign, you might say this:

"Blanket? Would you like to have your blanket?"

Always remember to give your child a chance to respond. Although she might not do more than coo or grunt, she is getting a feel for the rhythm of speech.

By repeating these words over and over as well as using them in context, you are actually giving your baby an advantage over many nonsigning children who are less likely to hear a word repeated as frequently. Before you know it, your child will first be signing and then speaking.

A Little or a Lot? It's Up to You

Different parents have different goals when it comes to signing. Some parents want to give their babies the ability to communicate through symbols while they are still preverbal. These parents will be satisfied if their babies can only express their basic needs with signs such as MILK, DIAPER, and EAT.

Other parents want to give their children communication assistance as they make their way through toddlerhood. The goal of these parents is to help their children to express not only their needs but their wants as well.

Finally, other parents hope to lay a foundation for continuing with sign language in the future. These parents want their children to acquire every sign they can so that they can go beyond the basic signs and learn to sign fluently as they get older.

E-ALERT

While your goals for your baby's future are important, do not let them get in the way of what you can teach her in the short term. Focusing too much on the big picture can detract from the little accomplishments that your baby reaches today.

No matter which type of parent you are, it is up to you to determine how much you want to sign with your child. If you are undecided, you might want to start out small and expand your goals as your baby becomes more proficient in sign. No matter how much signing you ultimately use with her, she will most likely be able to communicate earlier than many of her nonsigning peers, even if only to a small degree.

Signs for Baby's First Needs

8

From the day they are born, babies begin to express their needs. They know when they are hungry, and they know when they need a clean diaper. They want to let you know it, too. That desire to communicate is what makes the signs in this chapter the perfect introductory signs for your baby. Start with the basic words, and progress to some of the others as your baby gets older or as the need arises.

BABY FOOD SIGNS

There is little that excites a young baby more than a good meal. Whether it consists simply of milk or involves a bit of food, most little ones love to eat. That passion for nourishment will help encourage your baby to use the following signs. The fact that babies eat and drink multiple times throughout the day provides you with many opportunities to demonstrate the signs. After your baby comprehends the meaning of these signs, he will use them not only during the act of eating and drinking but also to signify his hunger or thirst.

The time will come when your baby will need signs beyond EAT and DRINK to express his desire for food. A child who wants applesauce, for example, will not be satisfied if he is offered cheese instead. As the variety of your baby's diet grows and his ability to sign improves, you can introduce him to specific food signs. In Chapter 12, you will find the signs for many of baby's favorite foods, such as BANANAS, MACARONI, and CRACKERS.

E-FACT

Although every baby is different, "ba ba" (for bottle) is frequently a third or fourth word in a baby's vocabulary. Which words typically rank higher? It should come as no surprise that "da da" (Daddy) and "ma ma" (Mommy) generally take the lead.

MILK

MILK (⊙ SEE DVD) is commonly one of the first signs used with babies. It resembles the act of milking a cow, and it will likely be exciting to your baby. After all, what preverbal baby would not want to communicate his desire for milk?

1. Bring your hand in front of your body and form it into a fist.
2. Open and close your fist demonstrating a squeezing motion.
3. You can also alternate an up-and-down motion to imitate the milking of a cow if you desire.

As you will have many opportunities throughout the day to demonstrate this sign, be sure to do so at every feeding— even in the middle of the night. You may be amazed at how quickly your baby picks up this sign. If you are unsure that your baby is actually signing, simply offer him a bottle or the opportunity to nurse. If he feeds eagerly, chances are he was trying to tell you something.

EAT

For babies who have graduated to baby food, EAT, as shown in **FIGURE 8-1**, is another highly motivating sign. It may not be the easiest one for your baby to sign perfectly, but he will likely adapt it to work for him.

FIGURE 8-1 *Eat*

1. Draw the tips of all of your fingers and thumb together as if operating a hand puppet with its mouth closed.
2. Bring your hand up to your mouth and touch your fingertips twice to your lips.

You may notice that your baby begins to point to his mouth with one or two fingers at mealtimes. If so, congratulations! He is signing! Give it time, and continue to model the actual ASL sign (unless you are practicing modified ASL). Eventually he will form it correctly.

E-SSENTIAL

Because infants still get the majority of their calories and nutrition from milk or formula, that is what they typically want when they are hungry. Do not be surprised if your baby only signs EAT while he is actually eating and MILK when he is hungry. In time, this will change.

DRINK

When your baby begins to use a cup, you may want to introduce the sign for DRINK, as shown in **FIGURE 8–2**. This sign should be fairly simple for your baby to sign.

1. **Cup your hand as if holding a glass.**
2. **Raise it up to your mouth as if drinking.**

Alternately, you can also introduce the sign for CUP (as described in Chapter 11) at this stage. If your child has already learned the sign for MILK, you may find that he uses MILK and DRINK interchangeably. MILK may become his sign of choice for juice, water, and any other beverage. Conversely, he may also use the sign for DRINK when requesting MILK. If you are able to understand what he is signing, respond to his request, but continue to model the correct sign. In time, your baby will be able to differentiate between the two signs.

SIGNS FOR BABY'S FAVORITE PEOPLE

Certain people invariably hold a special place in the hearts of most infants. Mothers and fathers, of course, usually rank highest on the list, but babies have a deep affection for all who play a role in their daily lives, including siblings. The signs in this section will provide a way for your little one to ask for the person he most wants to be with at any given moment. Prepare to have your heart melt the first time he makes the sign that represents you.

MOMMY

If you are a mother trying to use this sign with your child, it will be difficult to do so yourself. Your baby will likely not understand to what you are referring. Instead, someone else will have to demonstrate the sign each time your baby catches

FIGURE 8–2   *Drink*

sight of you (such as when you walk into the room or when you come home from work).

1. **Spread your hand open with your thumb pointing toward you.**
2. **Tap the tip of your thumb to your chin as shown in FIGURE 8-3.**

To further emphasize the meaning, be sure to say "mommy" or "momma" every time you or someone else forms it.

DADDY

The sign for DADDY, as shown in **FIGURE 8-4**, is very similar to the sign for MOMMY.

1. **Spread your hand open with your thumb pointing toward you.**
2. **Tap your thumb to your forehead.**

In the same way that it is difficult for a mother to model the sign for MOMMY to a child, it is equally difficult for a father to model the sign for DADDY. Someone else should make the sign whenever he enters the room. Again, be sure to reiterate this word verbally as you sign it.

FIGURE 8-3   *Mommy*

> ### E-ALERT
>
> The sign for MOMMY and the sign for DADDY are very similar. Your baby may confuse the two in the beginning. If you find that he signs for Mommy but really wants Daddy (or vice versa), give him to the parent he wants and then demonstrate the correct sign.

SIBLING SIGNS

When it comes to sibling signs, things can get complicated. For example, although you are signing to indicate "brother" and "sister," your baby probably knows them by their names. So should

FIGURE 8-4   *Daddy*

you say their names while signing their family titles? To further complicate matters, the sign for BROTHER and the sign for SIS-TER are remarkably similar. In fact, they both end the same. Therefore, you will want to be sure to emphasize the first part of each sign to help your baby differentiate between the two.

Ideally, your other children will be participating in signing with the baby as well. If so, you will want someone other than the siblings themselves to demonstrate the signs to your baby. If, however, your baby's siblings are not in the habit of signing with him, then it will actually be beneficial to have them make the signs themselves. This will cause your baby to associate these signs with the siblings they represent.

E-QUESTION

What if my baby has more than one brother or sister?

To distinguish one sibling from another, a bit of creativity may be necessary. If your other children have particularly short names, you may choose to spell them out. Otherwise, you might consider making the sign for BROTHER or SISTER and then adding the first initial of the child's name.

BROTHER

The sign for BROTHER (**⊙ SEE DVD**) is a two-handed motion that is fairly complex for a baby.

1. Imagine you are wearing a baseball cap. Reach up and grab the "visor" of the cap with your right hand.
2. Make the G hand shape with both hands.
3. Still holding the G hand shape, bring your right hand down and rest it upon your left.

Your baby will likely begin to understand its meaning long before he begins to sign it. In the meantime, your baby may simply point to or reach for his brother.

SISTER

The sign for SISTER (**◉ SEE DVD**) is another two-handed motion that may take some time to practice.

1. Form the A hand shape with your right hand and run it down your face from your cheek to your chin.
2. Form the G hand shape with both hands.
3. Bring your right hand down and rest it upon your left hand.

As with BROTHER, it may take weeks or months for your baby to begin forming this sign. Give it time, and eventually your baby will delight you by asking for his sister.

SIGNS OF REST AND RELAXATION

Babies and young children are often reluctant to go to bed. Therefore, you may be surprised at their willingness to let you know when they are tired. Either of these signs can be used to express a baby's desire to rest, though it is more accurate to use the sign for BED to refer to the piece of furniture, while the sign for SLEEP will refer to the act. You may find, however, that because of the simplicity of the sign, your baby starts to use the sign for BED to indicate sleep.

BED

The sign for BED, as shown in **FIGURE 8-5**, is familiar to most people and is easy for baby to form.

1. Tilt your head to one side.
2. Press both palms together in a "prayer" pose and bring up to your head.
3. Rest your head against your hands.

Another variation is to rest your head against the open palm of just one hand. Toddlers seem to love this sign and may

FIGURE 8-5 *Bed*

occasionally form it even when not tired. If your child forms the sign and it is not his usual bedtime or naptime, you may want to try cuddling with him for a bit to see if he is truly tired.

SLEEP

Although the sign for SLEEP (**O SEE DVD**) mimics the action of falling asleep, it is a complicated one for babies to learn. Your child may soon comprehend its meaning, but he may have difficulty forming the sign himself.

1. Spread your hand in front of your face, palm facing toward you.
2. Move your hand downward across your eyes, closing the fingers.
3. Your eyes should follow the motion of your hand and close to indicate that you are asleep.

As you sign with your baby, you can expect that he will create his own variations. Look for anything that resembles this sign so that you can react appropriately when he forms it.

SIGNS OF DISCOMFORT AND ILLNESS

Is there anything more disheartening as a parent than knowing that your child is upset, but not knowing exactly what the problem is? It is particularly distressing when your baby is ill or in pain and you don't know how to alleviate his discomfort. This is a source of major frustration for both you and your baby. The signs in this section will allow your baby to tell you when he is sick or when something hurts. As he discovers this newfound power of communication, he will likely take great comfort in it.

E-SSENTIAL

As your baby becomes proficient in these signs, he will probably begin to indicate which part of his body is causing him discomfort. For example, he may make the sign for PAIN and then point to his stomach to indicate a tummy ache.

Don't be discouraged if it takes a while for your baby to master these signs. They represent intangible concepts, and there are typically few opportunities to demonstrate them. However, if you practice these signs every time you get the chance, your child will eventually learn them.

PAIN/HURT

Introducing a baby to the sign for PAIN (⊙ **SEE DVD**) can be difficult because he will likely be distracted by the very pain to which you are referring.

1. Bring your hands in front of your body and point your index fingers at one another.
2. Twist your fingers in opposite directions.

One effective way to introduce this sign is to demonstrate it when you have hurt yourself. In addition, take advantage of small ouchies (such as a fall on the bottom or a light bump on the head) that your baby experiences. These minor incidents are not likely to be as distracting to your baby, but they will still allow him to grasp the concept of pain. Another opportunity for instruction is during teething, as it will occur frequently and last a while. There are not too many advantages to the pain of teething, but this is one of them.

HELP

Circumstances may arise when your child needs help in accomplishing a task. Whether it be getting a favorite toy off a just-out-of-reach shelf or opening a closet or cupboard, the sign for HELP can be a useful tool.

1. Spread your hand open in front of you, palm upward.
2. With your other hand, make a fist, extending your thumb upward.
3. Place the bottom of your fist on top of your palm and raise both hands upward.

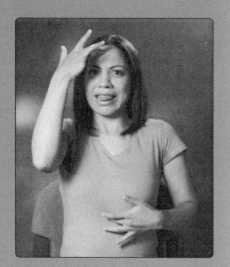

FIGURE 8–6 *Sick*

SICK

SICK, as shown in **FIGURE 8–6**, is a sign that is very easy to form but very difficult to comprehend.

1. **Touch your middle finger to your forehead.**

Additionally, your child could point to the area of the body that does not feel well, like his stomach. Unless your baby is frequently ill, however, you will have few opportunities to demonstrate it. Even then, it may take some time for your child to associate the sign with the feeling. For babies who are seldom sick, the days following routine immunizations are an ideal time to practice this sign.

POTTY SIGN

From early on, babies recognize that a dirty diaper causes some discomfort. When your child discovers that he can get a diaper changed by a seemingly magic wave of his hands, he will undoubtedly delight in making his request. However, don't be surprised if you occasionally end up changing a clean and dry diaper. Sometimes babies practice their signs just for fun.

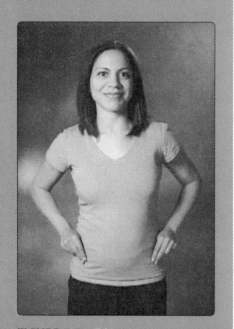

FIGURE 8–7 *Diaper*

DIAPER

The sign for DIAPER, as shown in **FIGURE 8–7**, comes from the act of pinning a diaper closed.

1. **Hold your hands in front of your waist with your fingers pointed downward.**
2. **Make a pinching motion with your index and middle fingers against your thumbs.**

This motion may seem foreign to your baby, so if you find that he is seemingly scratching at his diaper, he may actually be signing.

SIGNS FOR TRANSITIONAL OBJECTS

Transitional objects, also known as lovies, are items that a baby has formed a certain attachment to. These items offer a sense of well-being to a baby due to their familiarity, their smell, their feel, or a combination of all three. Common transitional objects include teddy bears, blankets, and pacifiers. If your baby has one of these lovies, you will most certainly want to study the signs in this section. As these objects are a source of comfort, most babies will take great joy in being able to ask for them as they wish.

TEDDY BEAR

Most commonly, the sign used for TEDDY BEAR, as shown in **FIGURE 8-8**, is actually the ASL sign for BEAR.

1. **Cross your arms across your chest.**
2. **Claw at your chest a few times as though you are a bear clawing.**

This is a fun one for young children to sign and once it is learned, it is likely to be frequently repeated. After your child seems to fully understand the meaning of this sign, feel free to also demonstrate it to him as the sign for a real bear. This will help him to make the connection between his toy and the animal.

FIGURE 8-8 *Teddy Bear*

BLANKET

The sign for BLANKET (**⊙ SEE DVD**) is one that will become quite familiar, and it is easy to learn.

1. **Hold your hands out in front of you as though you are holding a blanket with your fingertips.**
2. **Pretend to cover yourself with that blanket.**

This may be an easy sign for your baby to learn although you may not recognize it when he first attempts it. If you suspect that your baby is forming the sign for BLANKET, offer one to him and see if it appeases him. It is always better to assume your child is signing and react appropriately than to risk missing the opportunity for praise and acknowledgment.

PACIFIER

PACIFIER (**◉ SEE DVD**) is a two-motion sign that accurately represents the word it stands for, but it may be too complex for an infant.

1. **Rock your arms as if holding a baby.**
2. **With a closed fist, touch the tip of your thumb to your lips.**

If you are practicing modified American Sign Language, you might consider dropping the first half of this sign to make it simple for your baby to learn.

E-ALERT

Some babies confuse the signs for BOTTLE and PACIFIER. The signs are quite different, but because they both involve the act of sucking, some babies will use the sign interchangeably. If it is likely that your baby is hungry, he is probably requesting a bottle.

Many parents leave pacifiers easily accessible to their babies. If your baby is able to get to his pacifier without asking for it, or if he has devised another way of asking for it, you may choose to skip this sign altogether. It will be more beneficial to you and your child to focus on the signs that he needs and is most likely to use.

BALLOON

The sign for BALLOON that is widely used in baby-signing circles is the ASL sign.

1. **Put both hands in front of your mouth as if holding a balloon to your lips.**
2. **With your cheeks puffed up, pretend to blow up the balloon and move your hands outward to show the expansion of the balloon, as shown in FIGURE 8–9.**

In the end, your "balloon" should be completely blown up as indicated by the width between your hands.

FIGURE 8–9 *Balloon*

Signs for Parts of Baby's Day

A baby's day is usually filled with familiar routines. Bathing, getting dressed, and playing are all significant parts of her everyday life, and because these things occur so frequently, they can be great signs to introduce early. The signs in this chapter include many elements of a baby's typical day. Pick and choose the ones that are relevant to your child.

9

CHAPTER 9

SIGNS OF GETTING DRESSED

While babies often prefer to go au naturel, there will sometimes be reasons why they would want to communicate their desire to get dressed. Some babies have clear opinions on the clothes they want to wear. Other babies like the warm and secure feeling that being snugly dressed gives them. Many babies learn quickly that shoes or a coat can mean a trip outside.

These signs will likely come quickly to your baby, as you will have multiple times throughout the day to demonstrate them. If you find that you are having trouble remembering the sign for each article of clothing, consider posting a cheat sheet near your baby's changing table or any other place where you commonly dress her.

COAT

The sign for COAT (**◉ SEE DVD**) may sound a bit complicated, but it will probably come fairly quickly to you and your baby. The sign should look similar to actually pulling on a coat.

1. **Curl the fingers on both hands as if you are signing the letter A.**
2. **Bring your hands up and in front of your shoulders then down the length of your torso.**

Depending on where you live, you may have limited opportunities to demonstrate this sign. For instance, if you live in southern Florida and don a jacket a couple of days out of the year, you may have no need to use this sign.

E-SSENTIAL

The sign for COAT can actually be used for almost any sleeved outerwear, including jackets, windbreakers, trench coats, and suit jackets. To form the sign for RAINCOAT, simply sign RAIN (see Chapter 15) and then COAT. You may find, however, that your child associates the sign with one specific garment of clothing.

DRESS

The sign for DRESS (**○ SEE DVD**) is one that actually looks like what it represents.

1. Hold your hands in front of your chest with your fingers spread.
2. Move your hands down the length of your chest and then outward to indicate the skirt part of the dress.

Boys, of course, will have fewer opportunities to use this sign and therefore may not need it. If you do want to introduce this sign to your son, however, special occasions where people are dressed up are a good time to do so.

PANTS

This sign may take some getting used to for your child. Before she gets a good grasp of it, you may find that she simply pats at her legs to indicate PANTS (**○ SEE DVD**).

1. Open both hands with the palms facing each other. They should be about a half a foot apart, in front of one of your thighs.
2. Move both hands down each thigh, indicating the legs of a pair of pants.

There is another common ASL sign for PANTS that you might try if your baby is having trouble mastering the above sign. For this version, open your hands and rest them palm-down on your thighs. Then draw your hands up to your waist, bringing your fingertips and thumb together. This sign resembles the act of pulling up pants.

E-FACT

In American Sign Language, the sign for PANTS and the sign for SHORTS are entirely different and do not bear any resemblance to one another. To sign SHORTS, brush the fingertips of both hands along your hips. Make this motion twice to complete the sign.

FIGURE 9–1 *Shirt*

SHIRT

The sign for SHIRT, as shown in **FIGURE 9–1**, is a simple one that should come easily to your baby. In fact, she may even use it already without even knowing it.

1. **Use your index finger and thumb to pinch your shirt near the upper part of your shoulder.**
2. **Then tug at it a few times.**

This one will probably be a fun sign for your baby to make and she may do it already, even if she isn't trying to tell you anything.

SHOES

There's no place like home.
There's no place like home.
No, you won't be clicking the heels of your ruby slippers together to indicate SHOE as shown in **FIGURE 9–2**.

1. **Make a fist with both hands.**
2. **Tap the thumb sides of your hands together a few times.**

SHOE is one of several signs that use the motion of bringing both hands together in front of the body. Other such signs include those for BALL and MORE. You may have to be particularly observant in the beginning to determine which of these signs your child is trying to form.

FIGURE 9–2 *Shoes*

E-ALERT

Although there are specific signs for different types of shoes, it is unnecessary to model them for your baby, as this would likely confuse her and weigh her down with unnecessary signs. Additionally, she is unlikely to differentiate between shoe types at this point. Wait until she is older and then introduce the specific shoe signs, if you wish.

SIGNS OF PLAY

For many babies, playtime is the most fun and educational part of the day. Playing teaches cause and effect, nurturing skills, colors, shapes, and numbers. Your baby may be eager to demonstrate her desire to play, especially as she begins to prefer one toy to another. The signs in this section are relatively easy to form, making them great signs for younger signers to learn.

BALL

BALL, as shown in **FIGURE 9–3**, is a sign that will likely come naturally to your baby. In fact, she may already have her own version of it.

1. **Position your hands in front of you as if you are holding a large ball. At this point, your fingers should not be touching.**
2. **Bring your fingers together, tapping your fingertips together twice.**

Try showing your child balls in a variety of sizes and colors as you demonstrate the sign so that she will understand that the sign refers to all balls and not just one in particular.

DOLL

The sign for DOLL, as shown in **FIGURE 9–4**, will be easy to remember if you picture an old-fashioned cloth doll with a stitched X for the nose.

1. **Form the X hand shape, which is a fist that has your index finger held up and bent to form a hook shape.**
2. **Run the bent index finger down the length of your nose twice.**

You may find that your baby uses the sign for DOLL and the sign for TEDDY BEAR interchangeably or that she uses one

FIGURE 9–3 *Ball*

FIGURE 9–4 *Doll*

sign for both objects. If you are concerned about the accuracy of your baby's signs, just continue to demonstrate the correct sign for each object.

TOY

The sign for TOY (**◉ SEE DVD**) can be especially useful when teaching your baby to pick up her toys. In fact, you could even reserve this sign exclusively for cleanup time. In time, your child will understand that she must put her toys away when you demonstrate this sign.

1. **Form the T hand shape with both hands, which is a fist that has your thumb between your middle and index fingers.**
2. **Holding both hands in front of you, shake your hands.**

The sign for TOY is one that can be used for any toy. It may be difficult for your child to understand that each of her toys uses the same sign, so it is best left for general references to toys on the floor or in a toy box instead of for each individual toy.

> ### E-FACT
>
> The sign for PLAY is almost identical to the sign for TOY. Instead of using the T hand shape as you do in TOY, you simply shake your hands with the Y hand shape to indicate PLAY. If you find that your child is able to form one more easily than the other, you may want to use that one for TOY and PLAY.

SIGNS OF LEARNING

For babies, playing is learning, but these next signs pack a bigger educational punch than some other playtime activities. Your baby doesn't have to know that, though! Just keep on having fun and take pride in the fact that soon she will be demonstrating for you these signs of learning.

BOOK

Books are exciting to children of all ages, and babies are no different. Reading daily to your baby can improve her vocabulary and give her a better command of spoken English. The sign for BOOK, as shown in **FIGURES 9–5 AND 9–6**, actually looks like a book.

1. **Start with your palms together.**
2. **Now open your hands as if they were hinged on one side, like you are opening a book.**

FIGURE 9–5 *Book (Step One)*

MUSIC

The sign for MUSIC (**SEE DVD**) actually resembles the act of conducting.

1. **Hold one arm in front of your torso.**
2. **Move the other hand back and forth above your arm in a rhythmic fashion as if conducting.**

Don't be surprised if your baby makes this sign without the use of her still arm. She will likely pick up on the conducting part first, but the other may have to come later.

SIGNS OF GOOD HYGIENE

Hygiene is not likely to be on your baby's list of priorities. However, some children do love bath time. The following sign may be of interest to the little one who takes delight in this activity. It is easy to form and easy to remember.

FIGURE 9–6 *Book (Step Two)*

BATH

Babies either seem to love the water or hate it. The baby who loves to bathe will be eager to form this sign when she realizes that she can request bath time whenever she wants it. Those who are not as fond of the water will probably be very hesitant to form this sign, at least once they realize that it will result in a bath.

1. **Curl up the fingers of both hands, thumbs pointing up, and bring them to your chest.**
2. **Move your fists up and down your chest as if scrubbing your skin.**

The sign should resemble washing your chest. Check out the DVD to see it in motion.

E-ALERT

With so many water-related signs to learn, your baby may sometimes get the signs mixed up. It is best to only demonstrate one water sign at a time to minimize her confusion. In addition to BATH, other water signs include WATER (as in drinking or tap), SWIM, RAIN, LAKE, and PUDDLE.

If getting your child into the bathtub is a struggle, you may want to wait until after she is in the water to form the sign. It will not take very long before she associates the sign with the action, and seeing you make the sign might cause an unnecessary temper tantrum.

SIGNS OF ACTIVITY

Most babies love to move and groove, especially as they become more mobile. Not only do the signs in this section represent these moves, but they also mimic them. Your child will likely enjoy forming these signs and may do so often. Some babies may not bother with the signs at all and will simply demonstrate the action itself. See Chapter 16 for other signs of activity, such as WALK and RUN.

DANCE

Many toddlers have great fun dancing to their favorite music. With this sign, as shown in **FIGURE 9–7**, they can let you know when they want to groove.

1. **Extend your index and middle fingers downward, like legs.**
2. **Have the fingers dance across the palm of your opposite hand.**

Look for opportunities to demonstrate this sign, other than when your baby is dancing. Show your baby the sign whenever she sees dancing—in person, on television, or in books.

FIGURE 9–7 *Dance*

JUMP

The signs for JUMP (**○ SEE DVD**) and for DANCE are similar.

1. **As with DANCE, your index and middle fingers are acting as legs in this sign.**
2. **Simply have your fingers spring up off of the palm of your opposite hand.**

E-SSENTIAL

Want to make this sign a bit more fun? Make a game out of it. After a heavy rain, take your little one outside and look for puddles on the sidewalk. Point out the puddle and then demonstrate the sign for JUMP. Then help your child to jump over the puddle.

Because of this sign's similarity to DANCE, you may want to have one well established before introducing the other. As your child gets older and more skilled at signing, she will be better able to distinguish between two signs that are very much alike.

PAINT

PAINT (**O SEE DVD**) is a fun sign to form.

1. Using one hand to represent a canvas, hold it upright with your palm open.
2. Use your other hand like a paintbrush and make up and down strokes on your "canvas."

A fun way to reinforce this sign is by actually putting a paintbrush in your child's hand and allowing her to paint her other palm with it. To avoid a big mess, have her paint her hand with water.

Chapter 10

Signs for the People in Baby's World

Most babies are fascinated by people. They love to gaze at faces, study movements, and watch people interacting with one another. Because of this fascination, many babies will readily learn the signs for all kinds of people, above and beyond their immediate family members. By using the signs in this chapter, you will be giving your baby the ability to identify extended family, community helpers, and other familiar faces.

GENERAL PEOPLE SIGNS

Not everyone has a name—at least not to your baby. Still, he will likely enjoy identifying people based upon their age or gender. He will probably be able to spot the difference between a man and a woman and a baby and a child and want to acknowledge those differences. Because these age and gender variations may not always be apparent to younger babies, however, it may be more practical to introduce these signs when your baby enters toddlerhood.

FIGURE 10–1 *Baby*

BABY

Most babies seem to recognize their kinship to other babies. At the very least, they are fascinated by them. When your child develops an understanding for what a baby is, he will probably go out of his way to point them out to you. The sign for BABY, as shown in **FIGURE 10–1**, will help him to do that.

1. Put your arms in front of you and place one arm on top of the other, as if you were forming a cradle.
2. Sway your arms in front of you as if rocking a baby.

When you first set out to introduce this sign, try practicing it with a doll in your arms, particularly one that looks like a realistic baby. This will help your child to make the connection in his mind.

CHILD

The sign for CHILD (**⊙ SEE DVD**) is one that may not be very recognizable when your baby demonstrates it.

1. Pat the air in front of you, as if patting the head of a child.

Because it may appear that your baby is simply waving his arm, you may not realize that he is signing at first. Take note of any children who may be in your baby's line of sight and look for any possible resemblance to this sign.

BOY

To form the sign for BQY, as shown in **FIGURE 10-2**, it's helpful if you can visualize a little.

1. **Imagine you are wearing a baseball cap.**
2. **Reach up with one hand and grasp the visor of the cap twice. (The tips of all your fingers and thumb should be pressed together as if operating a hand puppet with its mouth closed.)**

FIGURE 10-2 *Boy*

That's it. You have just made the sign for BOY. While this sign is most commonly recognized as BOY it is actually a sign for males in general. It could be used to express GUY or MAN (in addition to BOY), though each of those has its own variation that is more commonly used and understood.

GIRL

The sign for GIRL, as shown in **FIGURE 10-3**, is meant to represent the tie of a bonnet.

1. **Form the A hand shape.**
2. **Run your thumb down from your cheek to your chin two times.**

FIGURE 10-3 *Girl*

E-FACT

Young boys and girls physically look the same and have a similar voice pitch. As a result, your baby may have difficulty differentiating between the two. If this is the case, you may want to simply use the sign for CHILD for all children, at least until he is a little older.

MAN

To do the sign for MAN (❍ **SEE DVD**), you'll need to reference Chapter 8 for the sign for DADDY (page 81). MAN is a simple variation on that.

1. Make the sign for DADDY by opening your hand with your fingers extended and tapping your thumb to your forehead. Imagine you're creating the look of a rooster.
2. Bring the open hand straight down and touch your thumb to your chest.

When demonstrating this sign for your baby, be sure not to use it in connection with men for whom your baby already has a sign (such as Daddy, uncle, or police officer). Instead, only use it with men who are strangers to your baby.

WOMAN

In the same way that the sign for MAN is an expansion on the sign for DADDY, the sign for WOMAN (❍ **SEE DVD**) is an expansion on the sign for MOMMY.

1. First sign GIRL by forming the A hand shape and running your thumb down your cheek.
2. Bring your hand straight down, open your fingers, and touch your thumb to your chest (like you did with MAN).

E-ALERT

When introducing the signs for MAN and WOMAN, be sure to demonstrate them in reference to people who have clear attributes of each gender. For example, a man with long hair might look like a woman to your child, while a woman with short hair might resemble a man. This could be confusing to a baby.

As with MAN, avoid modeling the sign for WOMAN in connection to women in your baby's life who already have a name (like Mommy or Grandma). Instead, point out women to your baby at the grocery store, walking down the street, or in any other public setting, and then model the sign for WOMAN. Do it often, and soon your baby will make the connection.

SIGNS FOR GRANDMA AND GRANDPA

While there is usually no one quite as special to a baby as Mommy and Daddy, Grandma and Grandpa come pretty close. As a result, your baby will probably be eager to name them, either verbally or with signs. Chances are that he will be able to sign their titles long before he can say them. You will likely find that even the most skeptical-of-signing grandparents will be thrilled the first time your baby signs GRANDMA or GRANDPA.

GRANDMA

Once you have learned the sign for MOMMY, the sign for GRANDMA (**☉ SEE DVD**) will be easy to pick up.

1. **Start by signing MOMMY with your thumb resting on your chin.**
2. **Move your hand away from your face, drawing two invisible humps in the air.**

At first, your baby may have some trouble managing to form the humps. He may simply move his hand away from his face in a straight line or in one big arc. He will probably figure out the humps eventually and in the meantime, Grandma will still be ecstatic.

CHAPTER 10

GRANDPA

In the same way that MOMMY and DADDY are similar signs, so are GRANDMA and GRANDPA. To make the sign for GRANDPA (**O SEE DVD**) you will start with the sign for DADDY.

1. Start by signing DADDY, with your thumb resting on your forehead.
2. Move your hand away from your face, drawing two invisible humps in the air.

E-SSENTIAL

Many signing families will tell you that their babies seem to think that all gray-headed men look alike. That is because these babies sign GRANDPA every time they see a man with silver hair. Interestingly enough, this mix-up seems to primarily occur with grandfathers and not grandmothers.

Many babies have more than one grandmother and grandfather. If this is the case with your little one, you may want to find a way to differentiate between them. One way is to add the grandparent's first or last initial to the sign. Therefore, Grandpa Simpson could be signed using GRANDPA and then S.

SIGNS FOR AUNT AND UNCLE

Aunts and uncles often have an active role in a baby's life. They are frequently called upon to babysit, and they usually make fun playmates. If your baby has more than one aunt or more than one uncle, however, things could get complicated. Consider attaching initials to the signs in the same way that you might with a grandparent, so that Aunt Sally would be signed AUNT + S.

There is a phenomenon that often occurs in families that may also help with this signing dilemma. In a family with young kids, names are invariably shortened as a child learns to talk. If there are children in the family who have shortened Uncle

Bobby's name to Bebe and Aunt Tonya's name to Yaya, then demonstrate those abbreviated names to your baby. Show him how to sign B + E for Uncle Bobby and Y + A for Aunt Tonya.

AUNT

If your baby has an aunt in his life, avoid introducing the sign for ANT until AUNT is well established. You wouldn't want his aunt to be offended if your baby refers to her as a bug. The sign for AUNT is shown in **FIGURE 10–4**.

1. **Form the manual alphabet letter A.**
2. **Hold it beside your cheek, and move your hand in a circular motion.**

FIGURE 10–4 *Aunt*

UNCLE

The sign for UNCLE, as shown in **FIGURE 10–5**, is similar in form to the sign for AUNT.

1. **Form the manual alphabet letter U.**
2. **Hold it beside your forehead, and move your hand in a circular motion.**

> ### E-FACT
>
> There is another commonly used and accepted ASL version of both AUNT and UNCLE. Instead of shaking your hand back and forth, you would make "draw" circles with your hand next to your cheek (for AUNT) or your temple (for UNCLE). The first part of each sign stays the same as in the other version.

FIGURE 10–5 *Uncle*

Because the sign for UNCLE requires that your baby extend his index and middle fingers, he may find it difficult while he is still young. Until he is well into toddlerhood, he may form the sign by extending *all* of his fingers and then shaking his hand at the side of his forehead.

SIGNS OF EVERYDAY PEOPLE

There are some people that your baby probably sees almost every day, aside from immediate family. While they may not play as active a role in your baby's life, they are still significant to your child. Therefore, give your little one the ability to label these people with signs. Just be sure not to use these signs simultaneously with others (such as signing NEIGHBOR and MAN for the same person) to avoid confusing your baby.

FRIEND

The sign for FRIEND, as shown in **FIGURE 10–6**, is meant to indicate the closeness of two friends.

1. **Bring both hands in front of the chest.**
2. **Link both of your index fingers together.**
3. **Reverse the placement of your hands and link your index fingers again.**

Because older infants and younger toddlers are just learning to socialize with their peers, the meaning of friendship will be lost on them. Therefore, consider using the sign for FRIEND to indicate "playmate." For instance, when you go to playgroup or to the park, use the sign for FRIEND to introduce your child to another baby. This will let your little one understand that the other baby is someone with whom he can play.

NEIGHBOR

NEIGHBOR (**⊙ SEE DVD**) is a two-motion sign that roughly combines NEAR and PERSON.

1. **Bring the palm of one hand together with the back of the other hand (this indicates nearness).**

FIGURE 10–6 *Friend*

2. With your palms facing each other in front of your torso, bring them down the length of your body to indicate person.

To help your child to understand the concept of neighbors, it will be especially helpful to demonstrate the sign when a neighbor is coming in or out of her house. If your baby associates the person with her house, he will start to grasp the fact that a neighbor is someone who belongs to the house next door (or across the street).

E-ALERT

Bringing the back of one hand to the palm of the other may take more coordination than your baby is able to demonstrate. Instead, you may find that he claps his hands together for the first part of this sign. Give it time, and continue to model the sign correctly. He will get it right eventually.

SIGNS OF GOOD HEALTH

Some babies love going to the doctor's office, and some babies hate it. Regardless, almost all babies are fascinated by the people they encounter there. Giving signed names to those people will help your baby to understand who they are, even if he still cannot understand how they help him. It is also a good way to let your baby know where he is going when it is time for an all-important trip to the doctor.

FIGURE 10–7 *Doctor*

DOCTOR

The sign for DOCTOR is shown in **FIGURE 10–7**.

1. Form the manual alphabet letter D with one hand.
2. Tap it to the inside wrist of the opposite hand to indicate checking for a pulse.

To help distinguish a doctor in your child's mind, point out the doctor's white coat, stethoscope, and other features that are singular to doctors. These visual clues will help your baby to identify doctors, therefore sealing the sign's meaning in his mind.

NURSE

NURSE, as shown in **FIGURE 10–8**, is very similar to DOCTOR.

1. **Form the manual alphabet letter N.**
2. **Tap it to the inside wrist of the opposite hand to indicate checking for a pulse.**

You may find that your baby has difficulty differentiating between a doctor and a nurse. Likewise, he may also have difficulty differentiating between the signs for DOCTOR and NURSE, due to their similarity. If you find that this is the case, try introducing one sign first and, when that one is well established, introducing the next sign.

FIGURE 10–8 *Nurse*

COMMUNITY HELPER SIGNS

There are a lot of people in baby's world, and it would be next to impossible to try to label them all. However, there are a few that your baby is most likely to see on a regular basis, as well as to be fascinated by when he does see them. Some of these signs are difficult to form, however, so these are good signs to modify if you are practicing modified American Sign Language. Once your baby learns the signs, he will take great delight in demonstrating them as much as possible.

FIREFIGHTER

Firefighters are some of the many civil servants your child may come in contact with. The sign for FIREFIGHTER is shown in **FIGURE 10–9**.

1. Open your hand, palm outward and fingers together.
2. Tap your forehead with the back of your hand.

It is most likely that the firefighters your child encounters will be riding on fire trucks. He will probably be so focused on the truck itself that he will miss the people inside. If you find that this is the case, consider taking your child to your neighborhood fire station to meet the firefighters. Most will be happy to talk to you and your child and they may even offer you a tour of the firehouse or fire engines.

FIGURE 10–9 *Firefighter*

POLICE OFFICER

Unlike many of the people signs in this chapter, the sign for POLICE OFFICER, as shown in **FIGURE 10–10**, is relatively easy to form.

1. Make the letter C with your right hand.
2. Tap it against the upper left side of your chest, as if indicating a police officer's badge.

Don't overlook security guards as good models for the POLICE OFFICER sign. They usually wear a similar uniform that, like that of a police officer, is adorned with a shiny badge. To your baby, a uniformed security guard and police officer will be one and the same. So be on the lookout for guards at the bank, grocery store, and other places that you and your baby frequent together.

FIGURE 10–10 *Police Officer*

Chapter 11

Eating Paraphernalia Signs

For a curious baby, mealtime is more than just an opportunity for nourishment. It is a chance to explore. Much of that exploration is not only of the food itself but also of the paraphernalia that goes with it. Many babies love to tap on their bowls with their spoons or tear up their napkins and let them waft to the floor. The signs in this chapter will allow your baby to identify these newfound toys that have her so captivated.

FIGURE 11–1   *Bowl (Step One)*

FIGURE 11–2   *Bowl (Step Two)*

SIGNS FOR BABY'S DISHES

Introducing your child to a bowl or a plate can be a messy endeavor. Plates often end up on the floor, and bowls often end up on baby's head. Although there is not much you can do to avoid this, you can try to distract your baby while she eats. One good way to do this is to introduce her to the following signs. If her little hands are busy signing, she won't have as much opportunity to dump out her dishes.

In addition to a distraction from mess making, these signs will provide your baby with labels for some very important everyday objects. She may also use these signs to indicate her desire to eat. Although the signs are simple, it may take a little time for your child to differentiate one from the other. Just be patient, and give her as many opportunities as possible to see and practice the sign.

BOWL

The sign for BOWL is an easy one to both remember and form.

1. **Cup both hands together in front of your body (see FIGURE 11–1).**
2. **Bring your hands up as if feeling the outside of a bowl (see FIGURE 11–2).**

An excellent way to illustrate this sign is by placing an actual bowl into your baby's cupped hands. This will help her to associate the sign with the object. Of course, it is best to do this with an empty bowl to avoid the inevitable mess that a full bowl would create.

Bowls come in a wide variety of sizes, colors, and even shapes. Allow your baby to look at and even handle these various bowls. This will broaden her concept of the word, and consequently, the sign. However, don't be surprised to find that your baby begins to label every container—including buckets, boxes, and bins—as a bowl. If that happens, applaud her efforts and then model the correct sign, if you wish.

E-FACT

The sign for POT is actually the same as the sign for BOWL. This may cause confusion for your child. For this reason, it might be best to show your child one meaning of the sign or the other, but not both. If you are practicing modified American Sign Language or a combination of home signs and ASL, however, you could alter this sign to better convey POT. One way to accomplish this would be to grip an imaginary handle with one hand after forming the sign for BOWL.

FIGURE 11–3 *Plate*

PLATE

Although there is more than one accepted version of the sign for PLATE, as shown in **FIGURE 11–3**, this version is an easy one for your baby.

1. Hold both hands in front of your body and spread your thumbs and index fingers wide.
2. Bring your extended fingers about a small plate's width apart.

To give your baby a visual demonstration, position your outstretched fingers around the rim of a plate to help promote understanding of the sign.

SIGNS FOR BABY'S UTENSILS

Utensils are often some of a baby's most prized possessions. A spoon or a fork can be used in so many creative ways. Many babies delight in pounding on their high-chair trays or on the bottom of a pot with their spoons. Forks and spoons frequently make their way to the floor after being flung from baby's hands.

And of course, most young children love to eat and quickly associate eating utensils with the food that they provide. With several opportunities throughout the day to demonstrate these signs, your baby will probably be signing them before you know it.

FORK

The sign for FORK (**◉ SEE DVD**) resembles the act of spearing a piece of food.

1. Form the letter V with your first and middle fingers.
2. With the tips of those fingers, tap the palm of your other hand twice as if your fingers are the tines of a fork and your palm is a plate.

For the sake of demonstration, you could actually hold a piece of food in your hand, tapping it with the first two fingers of the other hand.

E-ALERT

Don't be surprised to find that your baby does not learn the sign for FORK as quickly as she learns the sign for SPOON. Babies and toddlers generally use spoons more often than forks and therefore have more opportunities to see the sign modeled. You may also find that your baby uses one sign to indicate both fork and spoon.

To help your baby grasp the concept of a fork, try exposing her to different kinds of forks. Appetizer forks, carving forks, salad forks, and dinner forks all have slightly different appearances and can be used to help your child learn that tines are what identify a fork. Of course, any kind of fork can be hazardous to a baby, so be sure to supervise closely while allowing her to handle a fork.

SPOON

A spoon is probably the first eating utensil your baby will ever encounter, so she will be familiar with its shape early on. This familiarity will motivate her to want to demonstrate the sign.

1. Form the letter U with your index and middle fingers.
2. Curve those fingers slightly and use them to scoop imaginary food out of your other palm (as shown in **FIGURE 11–4**).

As with forks and bowls, try to expose your child to many different kinds of spoons, such as wooden spoons, slotted spoons, iced-tea spoons, and measuring spoons. Your baby will enjoy playing with the spoons and will gain a better understanding of both the object and the sign.

FIGURE 11–4   *Spoon*

SIGNS FOR DRINKING CONTAINERS

Whether from the bottle or the cup, babies love to drink. While some parents prefer to use signs for specific drinks such as milk, juice, or water, others find it easier to use signs for the containers. It is simply a matter of preference and practicality. For example, if your baby is particular about what she drinks, labeling each individual beverage might make more sense. That will allow her to specifically request milk or juice or water. However, if your baby is willing to drink just about anything you give her, it may be unnecessary for you to introduce her to any signs other than CUP and/or BOTTLE.

CUP

If you and your baby have already learned the sign for DRINK, the sign for CUP, as shown in **FIGURE 11–5**, will be easy.

1. With one hand, form the letter C.
2. Rest it in the open palm of your opposite hand.

FIGURE 11–5   *Cup*

This similarity between the signs means that you could allow your baby to use the signs interchangeably if you wish. After all, a baby who is signing for a cup is obviously requesting something to drink. With that in mind, you might find it unnecessary to use both signs with your child and instead may find it better to focus on only one.

E-QUESTION

Is there a separate sign for SIPPY CUP?

Not exactly. CUP is generally used to refer to any small drinking container. Some parents may choose to sign SIP and then CUP to differentiate, but it is unnecessary to do so.

Here is a simple way to expand your signing vocabulary, at least by one word. With just one step, you can transform the sign for CUP into the sign for GLASS. As with CUP, make the "C" hand shape and rest it in your palm. Then raise your C hand up to indicate a tall cup. Of course, you probably will not need the sign for GLASS as most babies and toddlers only drink from child-size cups.

BOTTLE

The sign for BOTTLE (**FIGURE 11-6**) is simple to form. Simply pretend your hand is a bottle and your thumb the nipple.

1. **Form a fist and extend your thumb upward (like the A hand shape).**
2. **Bring your thumb to your mouth, simulating the sucking of a bottle.**

Because a baby who is still drinking out of a bottle is usually drinking milk or formula, you might want to use the sign

FIGURE 11-6 *Bottle*

for MILK in lieu of the sign for BOTTLE. The exception to this is if you are breastfeeding. In that case, sign MILK while nursing and BOTTLE for supplemental feedings of juice or formula.

SIGNS OF CLEANLINESS

Is there a baby anywhere who appreciates the necessity of a postdinner wipe down? If so, those babies are few and far between. Most babies resist cleanliness and, in fact, love to make messes. Many babies even put up a fight when having a bib fastened around their necks. As with so many other things, distraction can be your best defense against these struggles. As you may be discovering, signing is a great distraction tool. Make clean-up time more fun by showing your baby the signs for NAPKIN and BIB.

BIB

The sign for BIB, as shown in **FIGURE 11–7**, is an iconic one.

1. Touch your fingertips to your lips as you do in the sign for EAT.
2. Form both hands into fists and "draw" a bib from your shoulders down to your chest with your hands.
3. Your hands should meet in the middle of your chest.

FIGURE 11–7 *Bib*

> ## E-FACT
>
> BIB is not a commonly used sign. You may even find that in some signing circles, the sign for NAPKIN is used in place of a sign for BIB. Because the sign is so iconic, however, there is really no reason not to use it with your child.

Because babies are such creatures of habit, even those who struggle against the bib may begin to look for you to sign BIB at the start of the meal. In fact, if you forget your baby's bib, don't be surprised if she signs and reminds you. This does not mean that she wants to wear the bib, of course. It simply means that she has become accustomed to the routine.

NAPKIN

NAPKIN, as shown in **FIGURE 11–8**, is a very easy sign to demonstrate as it simply mimics the act of wiping your mouth. Because toddlers often enjoy wiping their own mouths with a napkin, this sign may come naturally to many. In time, you will be able to instruct your child to wipe her own mouth by demonstrating the sign.

FIGURE 11–8   *Napkin*

1. **With your fingertips together, bring your hand up to your mouth.**
2. **Wipe your lips with your fingertips, as if using a napkin.**

Try practicing the sign using napkins of all different colors and materials such as paper napkins, paper towels, linen napkins, and terry-cloth napkins. Just pull out a napkin and wipe your mouth with it. Then demonstrate the sign. Once you have done it, pass the napkin to your child. This will give your baby the opportunity for extra signing practice, and she will enjoy handling the different cloths.

SIGNS OF PREPARATION AND SERVING

Is your toddler a little helper or a wanna-be chef? If so, she will probably enjoy learning these signs for food preparation and serving. You may find her following you into the kitchen and signing away as you prepare a meal. While this "assistance" in the kitchen may actually prove to be a hindrance, consider ways in which she really is able to help. Can she carry napkins to the table? Perhaps she can hold a spoon for you until you are ready to use it? By allowing her to help you, she will gain a deeper understanding of these signs, and you both will benefit from the quality time.

MICROWAVE

The sign for MICROWAVE (**⊙ SEE DVD**) is a two-motion sign, but it's simple to form.

1. "Draw" the outline of a microwave (a box shape) in the air with your fingertips.
2. Flick your fingers out toward each other as if you were trying to fling water off of your hands. (This motion represents the waves.)

While your child won't understand the concept of those waves, she will likely be curious about the microwave oven, particularly if you use it often.

STOVE

Though there are multiple accepted signs for STOVE, the one that you will find illustrated (**⊙ SEE DVD**) is one of the easier ones to form. The sign starts with the sign for COOK.

1. Pat the palm side of your right hand on the palm of your left hand, as if starting to clap.
2. Flip your right hand over and pat the back of it to your left palm.
3. Use your opened hands to outline the top and sides of the stove.

> ### E-ALERT
>
> It is common for babies and toddlers to gain interest in an object after they have learned the corresponding sign. When using a sign that indicates a stove or any other hazardous item, it is important also to remind your child that a stove is hot and should not be touched.

OVEN

The sign for OVEN (**⊙ SEE DVD**) is even easier than the sign for STOVE.

1. Hold your left hand out, palm down, in front of your body.
2. Run your right hand, with the palm up, under your left hand twice. This should resemble the act of placing something into an oven.

If you find that your child is confused by having two signs for the same appliance, you might want to use only the one that is easiest for her to form.

This is one instance in which it is not a good idea to use the actual object to demonstrate the sign. While it would be tempting to repeatedly open and close the oven door in an attempt to provide understanding, you do not want your child to think that opening the oven door is a game. In fact, if you have not done so already, now might be a good time to install a childproof oven lock for your baby's safety.

TABLE

The sign for TABLE, as shown in **FIGURE 11–9**, can also be used to indicate DESK.

1. Hold your left forearm horizontally in front of your body, with your right forearm hovering directly above it.
2. Bring your arms together twice. This represents resting your arms on a table or other flat surface.

FIGURE 11–9 *Table*

Remember that a table is not only used for mealtimes. If you and your child sit down at the table to color or put together a puzzle, be sure to model the sign for TABLE. This will help your child to recognize the table as a multifunctional piece of furniture.

Chapter 12

Food and Drink Signs

Babies who are well-established solid-food eaters will relish (pun intended) forming these signs. Because food and beverages are usually quite exciting to a young child, these are good early signs to choose.

CHAPTER 12

BEVERAGE SIGNS

From the time they are old enough to hold a bottle or a sippy cup, most babies want to carry a beverage with them everywhere they go. It's a good thing, too, because babies and toddlers are very active creatures who need a lot of fluids to keep them hydrated. Understanding when your child is thirsty, however, can be a challenge. The signs ahead will not only alert you to your baby's thirst but also help you discern what kind of drink he wants.

JUICE

If you know the sign for DRINK, as shown in Chapter 8, you will have no trouble learning the sign for JUICE (**O SEE DVD**).

1. **Form the sign for DRINK. (Cup your hand as if holding a glass. Raise it up to your mouth as if drinking.)**
2. **Finger-spell the letter J.**

If you want to specify a particular flavor of juice, such as apple juice or orange juice, form the sign for the fruit, and follow it with the letter J.

When you first introduce the sign for JUICE to your child, he may use it as a generic request for something to drink. In fact, you may discover that he uses it interchangeably with other beverage-related signs, including MILK, CUP, or DRINK. If you want your baby to have the ability to specify his drink choice, just continue to model the sign for each drink. He will eventually be able to differentiate between them.

WATER

The sign for WATER, as shown in **FIGURE 12–1**, is one that many children learn easily. This can be attributed to the fact that there are many opportunities to demonstrate the sign, and it represents something that is often exciting to young children.

1. **Form the letter W with your fingers.**
2. **With your fingers facing to the side, tap them to your chin.**

FIGURE 12–1 *Water*

> ### E-FACT
>
> Did you know that "water" is an early spoken word for some babies, usually emerging as "wa-wa"? If your baby begins to say the word, he may drop the sign. If you want him to retain his signing skills into childhood, it is important that you continue to model the sign every time he encounters water.

Babies like to splash in the sink, stomp in puddles, and play in the bath. All of these give you the opportunity to reinforce the sign. Of course, with so many purposes for water, it may not be clear what your baby is asking for when he signs it. Is he thirsty? Does he hear running water? Would he like to take a bath? As with so many other signs, it is important to read this sign in context. That should give you clues to the sign's meaning.

FRUIT SIGNS

Fruit is a popular treat among the stroller set. It's sweet, it's sticky, and it can often be mashed into the hair. What's not to love? Introduce to your baby the signs for his favorite fruits, and it won't be long before he is requesting them at meal or snack times. Does your baby have a penchant for a fruit that is not listed here, such as mango or kiwi? You will find a variety of resources in Appendix A of this book to help you find even the most exotic of signs.

APPLE

An apple a day may not actually keep the doctor away, but it does make a healthy snack for you and your baby. Full of fiber and vitamins, apples are a sweet treat that most children enjoy. The sign for APPLE (⊙ **SEE DVD**) is an easy one.

1. **Make a fist with your right hand.**
2. **Touch the knuckle of your right index finger to your cheek and twist your hand.**

BANANA

BANANA, as shown in **FIGURE 12–2**, is a fun sign to form.

1. **With one hand in front of you, extend your index finger upward to represent a banana.**
2. **Use your other hand to peel the "banana."**

Peeling a banana in front of your baby may help to reinforce this sign. Of course, you will not be able to sign and peel at the same time. So peel the banana in your baby's presence and then cut it up and serve it to him. While he eats, demonstrate the sign.

FIGURE 12–2 *Banana*

E-SSENTIAL

Introducing the sign for BANANA presents you with an excellent opportunity to model another fun sign: MONKEY. A great way to do this would be to find a picture in a book (think *Curious George*) or on the Internet of a monkey eating a banana. Then model the signs for each.

GRAPES

The sign for GRAPES (**⊙ SEE DVD**) is a complex one to form.

1. Hold your left forearm in front with your hand bent at the wrist.
2. Spread out the fingers on your right hand and bend them slightly and touch them to the top of your left wrist.
3. Lift your right hand, keeping your fingers in the same bent position and move the entire hand down an inch or so at a time. The fingers are used to represent the clusters of grapes in a bunch.

ORANGE

The sign for ORANGE (**⊙ SEE DVD**) represents the act of squeezing orange juice.

1. Form one hand into a fist.
2. Bring the thumb side of your closed fist to your mouth.
3. Open and close your hand a few times as if squeezing an orange.

VEGETABLE SIGNS

Chances are good that it is a struggle to feed your child his veggies. Make a game out of it by showing him these signs.

CARROT

The sign for CARROT, as shown in **FIGURE 12–3**, is a fun and easy one for baby to form.

1. Form the letter A hand-shape with your right hand.
2. Extend the index finger of your left hand and rub down the length of it with your right hand. (This rubbing motion represents peeling a carrot.)

FIGURE 12–3 *Carrot*

A great way to help your child associate the sign with a carrot is to peel carrots in his presence. As you do so, explain to him what you are doing and show him the peel after it comes off of the carrot. Even if you usually buy peeled baby carrots, consider picking up one or two full-sized carrots as a teaching tool for your baby.

E-ALERT

The sign for CARROT and the sign for GREEN BEAN are quite similar. This could cause some confusion for your baby as he learns the signs and some confusion for you as you decipher them. Be sure to avoid introducing the two signs at the same time, and try to emphasize the motion of the right hand in each.

CORN

The sign for CORN (**● SEE DVD**) is a simple one.

1. **Using both hands, pretend that you are holding a corncob up to your mouth.**
2. **Rotate the imaginary cob as if eating around it.**

The sign is a good representation of corn on the cob, but doesn't make as much sense for corn *off* the cob. In fact, your child may initially have trouble associating corn on the cob with the corn kernels on his plate. Just be sure to be consistent in modeling the sign, no matter what form of the vegetable you are serving.

GREEN BEANS

The sign for GREEN BEAN (or string bean), as shown in **FIGURE 12–4**, is formed like so.

1. Hold your left hand in front of your body with the index finger pointing to the right.
2. With your other hand, grasp the tip of the index finger of your left hand and twist, almost as if trying to snap the end off of the bean pod.

Unless you have a garden or purchase your vegetables from a farmer's market, you probably buy your green beans precut and frozen or in a can. If you have a farmer's market in your area or an extensive produce section at your local grocery store, consider picking up some whole green beans to demonstrate snapping off the ends.

FIGURE 12–4 *Green Bean*

PEAS

When you are ready to sign PEA (**⊙ SEE DVD**), keep that left index finger extended as you did with GREEN BEAN.

1. Hold your left hand in front of your body with the index finger pointing to the right.
2. Use your right index finger to touch your extended finger three or four times as if you are pointing out peas in the pod.

This is a great opportunity to incorporate a counting lesson in with signing practice. Each time you touch your index finger, count out loud. Likewise, if you show your child actual peas in a pod, be sure to count them, too.

POTATOES

The sign for POTATO (**○ SEE DVD**) is similar to the sign for FORK.

1. Form the letter V with your first and middle fingers.
2. Ball up the opposite hand into a fist.
3. Jab the fist with the two fingers of the other hand. (This represents spearing a potato with a fork.)

Interestingly enough, the sign for POTATO is almost identical to the sign for IRELAND. In fact, some American Sign Language speakers use the signs interchangeably. The reason for the similarity in signs is due to the fact that potatoes have long been a staple food source in Ireland.

SIGNS FOR LUNCH AND DINNER MEATS

Although there are countless kinds of meats, the ones represented in this section are commonly favorites among young children. If your child has an adult palate, you may need additional meat signs, such as pork, veal, or lamb. As with exotic fruit signs, if there is a particular meat sign that you would like to use with your baby that has not been included in this book, be sure to check out the resources in Appendix A.

CHICKEN

Although chicken is a favorite food for many toddlers, the sign for it, as shown in **FIGURE 12–5**, can be problematic. The sign for CHICKEN and the sign for BIRD are identical.

1. Bring one hand up to your mouth and press the index finger and thumb together (the remaining fingers should be tucked in to the palm).
2. Snap your thumb and index finger open and closed in front of your mouth, as if you have a beak.

FIGURE 12–5 *Chicken*

If you use the sign for both, your child may have trouble reconciling the flying creature in the air to the lifeless mass on his plate. Of course, this lack of understanding may well beat the alternative. It might be upsetting for a young child to realize what he is actually eating.

E-SSENTIAL

Because chicken is the type of poultry a child is most likely to eat on a regular basis, consider using this sign for any other poultry your child encounters. There is no reason to bog him down with the signs for TURKEY, HEN, or DUCK if he will only rarely, if ever, eat those birds.

Eventually, of course, all meat-eating children have to learn where their dinners come from. But this is a lesson that can generally wait until a child is much older.

HAMBURGER

The sign for HAMBURGER (**◉ SEE DVD**) represents the act of shaping a hamburger patty in your hands.

1. **Pretend you are holding a ball of ground beef in your left hand and cup your right hand over it.**
2. **Switch the imaginary ground beef to your right hand, cupping your left hand over it.**

If your child only sees the finished product, he may not readily make the connection between the sign and the burger. To help him to understand, let him watch the next time you make hamburgers or turkey burgers. Explain each step of the process, and show him what you are doing when you form the ball of meat and smash it flat.

HOT DOG

The sign for HOT DOG (● **SEE DVD**) is actually intended to represent a chain of linked sausages or wieners. These days, of course, most people buy their hot dogs in a plastic wrapped package of eight. So while it might be fun to try to find a chain of wieners at a butcher shop in order to give your baby a visual understanding of the sign, that demonstration will probably mean little to your child.

1. Hold your hands in front of you as if grasping the handlebars of a bicycle.
2. Open them slightly and move them apart a couple of inches and grasp again.
3. Do this one more time to complete the sign.

SIGNS FOR MEALTIME FAVORITES

There are some foods that babies and toddlers just love to eat. It usually takes almost no cajoling to get a child to eat these foods. Therefore, your baby may be highly motivated to learn and use these signs. For this reason, they may be good food signs to introduce to your baby early on. Signs like MACARONI are especially good for toddlers who are learning to speak but have not yet been able to master multisyllabic Italian words.

CEREAL

There are actually a couple of accepted American Sign Language signs for CEREAL. The one that will probably be the easiest for your baby to form is shown in **FIGURE 12–6**.

1. Hold your left hand in front of your body, palm up.
2. Use your right first and middle fingers to "scoop" something out of your palm and bring it to your mouth.

FIGURE 12–6 *Cereal*

CHEESE

The sign for CHEESE (● **SEE DVD**) might make you think of squishing a bug.

1. Bring the heels of both hands together.
2. Rotate them back and forth a few times as if mashing something between your hands.

The sign is actually intended to represent squeezing the excess liquid out of freshly made cheese.

EGG

The sign for EGG (● **SEE DVD**) is very simple.

1. Extend the first two fingers of both hands to form the letter U.
2. Bring your extended fingers together to form an X in front of your body.
3. Pull your hands away from each other and down toward the floor.

The sign should resemble cracking an egg into a bowl.

PEANUT BUTTER

The sign for PEANUT BUTTER (● **SEE DVD**) combines the signs for PEANUT and BUTTER.

1. Put the pad of your thumb behind your top front teeth.
2. Pull it outward a few inches from your body. This is the sign for PEANUT.
3. Next, hold your left palm out in front of you.
4. Run the tips of your first two fingers on your right hand over your left palm as if spreading something on your palm. This is the sign for BUTTER.

Let your child watch as you spread peanut butter on bread. If you feel particularly ambitious, offer him a plastic knife or even a spoon and allow him to spread the peanut butter on the bread. While he spreads, be sure to demonstrate the sign.

> **E-ALERT**
>
> Some children are highly allergic to peanuts. For this reason, the American Academy of Pediatrics recommending waiting until a child is at least one year old before offering him peanut butter. If he has a history of allergies or has family members with food allergies, the AAP suggests holding off on peanut butter until three years of age.

MACARONI

Once your baby gets the hang of the sign for MACARONI (see **FIGURE 12-7**), don't be surprised if he signs it at every meal.

1. Hold both hands in front of you with index fingers and thumbs extended.
2. Narrow the space between the index finger and thumb of each hand to approximately the width of a noodle.
3. Outline a macaroni noodle in front of your body.

Although a baby cannot live on macaroni alone, give it to him when he asks as often as possible, particularly when he first learns the sign.

FIGURE 12-7 *Macaroni*

SIGNS FOR SNACKS

Many babies and toddlers would probably choose to limit their diets to cookies and crackers if they could. While that can be problematic when trying to encourage your child to eat other foods, it is very helpful while introducing these signs. It shouldn't take long for your baby to figure out that forming these signs will get him a cookie or a cracker when he asks. Of course, if he asks all the time, it may be a great opportunity for you to demonstrate the signs for NO (page 195) or ALL GONE (page 194).

COOKIE

To form COOKIE, as shown in **FIGURE 12–8**, imagine that your left hand is cookie dough that has been rolled out flat.

1. **Hold your left palm upward in front of your body.**
2. **Place the fingertips of the right hand onto the left palm as if the right hand was a round cookie cutter.**
3. **Rotate the right hand on the palm of your left hand as if cutting out a cookie.**

FIGURE 12–8 *Cookie*

Want to bring this sign home for your child? Make cookies and allow him to help you cut them out of the dough with cookie cutters. As an added bonus, you can make the cookies in a variety of shapes, giving your child a bonus lesson in shapes.

CRACKER

CRACKER, as shown in **FIGURE 12–9**, may be a little difficult for a baby or toddler to form, but with a little practice it will surely become a favorite sign.

1. **Cross your left forearm over your chest so the elbow faces forward.**
2. **Form your right hand into a fist.**
3. **Brush your left elbow with your right fist.**

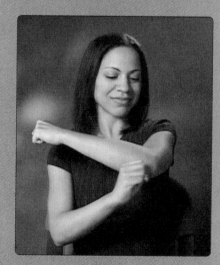

FIGURE 12–9 *Cracker*

It is acceptable for your forearm to cross your chest diagonally, as in the picture, or horizontally across your abdomen.

E-FACT

The right cracker can actually be a nutritious addition to your child's diet. Look for crackers that are made with whole grains, are high in fiber, and are low in sugars. Your child will probably be just as happy to munch on them as on any other cracker.

This sign may be difficult at first, so look for variations on this sign from your child. He may simply pat his elbow or touch his shoulder. If you are unsure that he is really signing CRACKER, just ask him. An excited reaction will be your answer.

Chapter 13

Animal Signs

Is your baby fascinated by animals? Does she chase after the family pet or reach for the creatures at the zoo? Kids of all ages, including infants and toddlers, are usually intrigued and delighted by animals. In this chapter, you will learn to form the signs for some of the most popular animals among the baby and toddler crowd. You will also find great activities to help your child learn them.

Farm animals are typically some of babies' favorite furry friends. If there is a petting farm in your area, consider taking your child for a visit. She will love feeling the different textures of the animals and watching them as they eat and play. If that option is not available to you, perhaps you could check out a picture book on farm animals from the library. Another fun way to demonstrate these signs is by using them while you sing "Old McDonald Had a Farm." Not only will your child learn the signs, she will also learn the animal sounds.

FIGURE 13–1 *Cow*

COW

The sign for COW, as shown in **FIGURE 13–1**, is meant to indicate the horn on a cow.

1. **Extend the thumb and pinky finger of one hand, as if making the Y hand shape.**
2. **Touch your thumb to your temple and twist your wrist upward.**

If you want to show your child a cow up close, take a car ride into the country. You will likely come across cattle farms with cows grazing in the fields. Point out the different colors that cows come in for a quick lesson in color.

HORSE

HORSE (**◉ SEE DVD**) is similar to the sign for COW and is meant to represent the ear of a horse.

1. **Extend your first and middle fingers, as if forming the U hand shape.**
2. **Extend your thumb and touch your thumb to your temple.**
3. **Waggle your fingers forward and back up a few times.**

It is interesting to note that the signs for HORSE and RAB-BIT (page 142) are alike. For this reason, it is best to introduce the signs one at a time to help avoid confusion. Pick the one that your child seems most interested in to start with. After that one is well established, move on to the next sign.

E-FACT

Is your child clamoring to ride a horse? Children as young as five years of age can be taught to ride a horse by themselves, and most riding stables will permit them to do so at that age. Prior to age five, a child can often safely ride on a horse with an adult.

PIG

The sign for PIG, as shown in **FIGURE 13–2**, represents slop dribbling down a pig's chin.

1. Rest your chin on the back of your hand.
2. Bend and unbend all four of your fingers in unison a few times.

SHEEP

The sign for SHEEP (**SEE DVD**) is somewhat complex but makes sense.

1. Hold your left forearm in front of your body with your palm upward.
2. Using your right hand, make the V hand shape to represent scissors.
3. Use your "scissors" to pretend to clip wool from your left wrist.
4. Move your right hand up a few inches and clip the wool again.
5. Repeat this step up the inside of the forearm.

FIGURE 13–2 *Pig*

Explain to your child that wool is sheared from sheep in the same way that people get a haircut. Look for pictures or videos of this process to illustrate it. Reassure your baby that the "haircut" does not hurt the sheep.

SIGNS OF FAVORITE PETS

If you have pets in your home, chances are good that your baby adores them. Unfortunately, your pet may not adore your baby. Many babies point at, or motion toward, pets in an effort to acknowledge them. The signs in this section will give them a way to acknowledge the pet's presence and to alert you to it, as well. The signs for some other popular pets, including fish, birds, and rabbits, are illustrated elsewhere in this chapter.

CAT

The sign for CAT, as shown in **FIGURE 13–3**, is relatively simple.

1. **Bring your thumb and your index finger up to your cheek, very close to your nose. At this point, the fingers should not be touching.**
2. **Move your fingers out to the side and pinch them together (your remaining fingers will be extended). It should look like you are stroking whiskers on your face.**

FIGURE 13–3 *Cat*

> ## E-ALERT
>
> Although the notion of a cat sucking the breath out of a baby is nothing more than an old wives' tale, a cat could conceivably lie across a baby's face, rendering her unable to breathe. For this reason, it is best to keep a cat out of a sleeping baby's room.

If your cat will allow it, stroke his whiskers in your child's presence and then form the sign. This should help your child to make the connection between the cat and the sign. Try not to aggravate your cat, though. With a baby in the house, he is probably aggravated enough as it is.

DOG

DOG (**⊙ SEE DVD**) is a simple sign, though it requires two motions.

1. Pat your thigh with your open hand.
2. Snap your fingers twice.

If you have a dog in the house, the sign may cause him to come running. This would actually be helpful in reinforcing the sign for your child.

Children who have pet dogs are particularly trusting of all dogs, including neighborhood strays. Try to instill a sense of respect in your child for dogs, and teach her not to touch them without permission. You don't want her to be afraid of them, but you also don't want her to inadvertently approach an aggressive dog.

SIGNS OF NEIGHBORHOOD ANIMALS

As a baby begins to observe the outside world, some of the most fascinating things she will encounter are animals. These outdoor creatures are generally quick and sometimes make little noise. It may be hard for your baby to get a good look at them. If you find that your baby is interested in a particular animal, but it continuously escapes her line of sight, seek out photographs and illustrations of the animal to show to your child.

BIRD

As you may have read in Chapter 12, the signs for BIRD and CHICKEN are identical (**⊙ SEE DVD**).

1. Bring one hand up to your mouth and press the index finger and thumb together (tuck the remaining fingers into the palm).
2. Snap your thumb and index finger open and closed in front of your mouth, as if you have a beak.

If you plan to use this sign for BIRD, it might be best to avoid using it for CHICKEN, at least until your child is old enough to understand what she is eating.

> ## E-SSENTIAL
>
> Birds provide many opportunities for learning. You can use them to teach your child about flight, about worms, and about eggs. Be sure to take advantage of the many colors that birds come in to give your child a lesson on colors, as well. Emphasize the red of the cardinal or the black of the crow.

Because birds are so often heard and not seen, be sure to demonstrate the sign for BIRD every time you and your baby hear one chirp. Your child will soon associate the bird, the chirp, the sign, and the spoken word with one another.

RABBIT

The sign for RABBIT, as shown in **FIGURE 13–4**, is similar to the sign for HORSE.

1. **Form the U hand shape with your thumb extended.**
2. **Bring your hand up to the top of your head so that the heel of your hand is touching your forehead.**
3. **Waggle the first two fingers of your hand back and forth a couple of times.**

If you happen to have a pet rabbit, then you will have many opportunities to demonstrate this sign. If not, a rabbit can sometimes be hard to spot. Consider using pictures in books or stuffed toy rabbits to illustrate this sign.

FIGURE 13–4 *Rabbit*

SQUIRREL

The sign for SQUIRREL, as shown in **FIGURE 13–5**, is one most children eagerly try to form.

1. Curl your fingers into fists with your first and middle fingers raised up a bit.
2. Bring the heels of your hands together, one on top of the other, and tap your first two fingers against each other twice.

This is a good sign to use, as babies are frequently amused by squirrels.

FIGURE 13–5   *Squirrel*

SIGNS OF ANIMALS IN THE WATER

A great place to model the signs for these water animals is at an aquarium, pet store, or even a neighborhood pond. If those options aren't available to you, take inventory of your child's bath toys. You may discover that you've got everything you need right in your own bathtub.

FISH

There is a more commonly used, two-handed motion to indicate FISH, but the single-hand motion will probably be easier for your child to master (**O SEE DVD**).

1. Extend your hand as if offering a handshake.
2. Make your hand "swim" in a zigzag motion like the tail of a fish.

E-ALERT

If you plan to use this sign for both the goldfish in the fish bowl and the fish on your baby's plate, your baby may be confused. Consider using one form of the sign or the other, but not both, at least until your child is older and able to understand what she is eating.

Fish are beautiful creatures and come in a wide variety of colors and sizes. Use this to your child's educational advantage. Point out the big fish versus the little fish and the shiny fish versus the dull fish. Show your child the fish with stripes and then the fish with spots, and the blue fish in comparison to the white fish.

FROG

The sign for FROG, as shown in **FIGURE 13-6**, represents a frog's vocal sac that expands when it croaks.

1. **Rest your chin on the back of your hand with your fingers curled into a fist.**
2. **Flick your index and middle fingers outward twice to complete the sign.**

It is not always easy to encounter a frog in your neighborhood. If you want to try, go outside on a warm damp evening with a flashlight. Look for frogs near puddles, ponds, rocks, and even in the wet grass.

FIGURE 13-6 *Frog*

TURTLE

The sign for TURTLE (**❍ SEE DVD**) indicates a turtle coming out of its shell.

1. **Form the A hand shape, and hold it in front of your body with the thumb on top.**
2. **Use your other hand to cover up the A hand shape.**
3. **Wiggle your thumb back and forth a couple of times to indicate a turtle's head peeking out of its shell.**

After showing your child a turtle, either in person or in pictures, try playing this game to help your child to understand that a turtle does not go away when he retreats into his shell, but that he is simply hiding. Take a blanket and wrap it around your shoulders and neck with just your head peeking out. Tell your child that you are going to go into your shell like a turtle and then cover up your head with the blanket. Quickly re-emerge and then let her have a turn playing the turtle.

E-FACT

The sale of turtle hatchlings that are fewer than four inches in length is prohibited in the United States. This ban was enacted in the 1970s as a way to reduce instances of salmonella infection in children, who are likely to put small turtles into their mouths.

SIGNS AT THE ZOO

The zoo is a popular destination for children of all ages, and there is usually something for everyone there. There are many different animals at the zoo; the ones included in this section are those that young children frequently find most fascinating. Before planning your next trip to the zoo, introduce these signs using pictures of the animals. When you point out these animals at the zoo, you may be delighted to find your child forming the corresponding signs.

ELEPHANT

To sign ELEPHANT (**◔ SEE DVD**) you will simply make a motion to demonstrate the elephant's trunk.

1. Touch the back of your hand to your mouth and nose.
2. Move your hand outward from your face and down to show the length of the trunk.
3. At the end of the "trunk," raise your hand back up slightly to indicate the curl of the trunk.

A fun and productive game that you can play with your toddler is elephant cleanup. Using the basic idea of the sign for ELEPHANT, form a trunk with your arm. Use your "trunk" to pick up toys off the floor and deposit them into a toy box. You may pick up more toys than your child, but isn't that what usually happens anyway?

GIRAFFE

The sign for GIRAFFE (**⊙ SEE DVD**) depicts a giraffe's long, long neck.

1. **Touch the bottom of your neck with your thumb and index finger.**
2. **Continue holding your fingers in that position, but raise your whole hand up the length of your neck.**

It is really difficult for a child to grasp just how tall a giraffe truly is without seeing one in person. If you can arrange a trip to the zoo to see this towering creature, your child will get a better understanding of its height.

MONKEY

Have you ever pretended to be a monkey? If so, you probably signed it without even realizing it. MONKEY as shown in **FIGURE 13–7**, is formed by simply scratching your sides twice.

FIGURE 13–7 *Monkey*

1. **Put both hands on the sides of your torso.**
2. **Scratch upward on your torso two times.**

Your baby will undoubtedly find it funny to watch you parading around like a monkey. Use this to your advantage by doing silly dances and making goofy faces. This will probably inspire your child to join in on the fun.

E-QUESTION

Are there different signs for each type of primate?

Most American Sign Language speakers use the same sign for MONKEY, CHIMPANZEE, and ORANGUTAN. However, the sign for GORILLA is made by thumping the chest alternately with both fists, mimicking the actions of a gorilla

TIGER

TIGER, as shown in **FIGURE 13–8**, is another sign that imitates the actions of the animal it represents.

FIGURE 13–8 *Tiger*

1. Bring your hand up in front of your face with your fingers bent inward like claws.
2. Pull your hand from the middle of your face to the side.
3. Repeat the motion to finish the sign.

Babies will sometimes confuse tigers and lions with domestic cats, particularly if they have a pet cat at home. If your child signs CAT upon seeing a tiger, acknowledge that it is, indeed, a big cat and then go on to sign TIGER.

SIGNS OF BUGS

They're creepy and they're crawly, and for many parents, they may be downright icky. But for kids, bugs are a lot of fun. They are small and they move in ways that people simply can't. And young children don't find them yucky or disgusting. On the contrary, older infants and toddlers may try to pick up the bugs that they see, and some will even try to eat an insect or two. This exploration is usually harmless, so even if you find it disgusting, try to allow your child to experience bug-related hands-on learning.

ANT

The sign for ANT (**○ SEE DVD**) is usually the same sign used for any generic bug.

1. Touch your extended thumb to the tip of your nose.
2. Curl your ring and pinky fingers into the palm.
3. Extend your index and middle fingers so they are standing upright.
4. Bend them downward twice to form the sign.

> ### E-FACT
>
> One species of red ant, known as the fire ant, is aggressive and has a venomous sting. The sting from a fire ant causes pain and itching and can even cause injection-site infections. Some children are severely allergic to the sting of a fire ant, so it is best to not let your child get too close to these ants.

Here is a fun activity that will give you the opportunity to form the sign for ANT. Finely crush a couple of graham crackers or cookie pieces. Take them outside and sprinkle them in a small area away from your house. Wait a few minutes and then observe the crumbs. You will probably find black ants teeming around the area and carrying crumbs on their backs. Point them out to your child, and let her observe or even follow the ants as far as possible.

BUTTERFLY

The sign for BUTTERFLY, as shown in **FIGURE 13–9**, is one that you may have formed without realizing that you were signing.

1. Spread your hands open with your palms facing you and cross your arms at the wrist.
2. Link your thumbs together.
3. Bend your fingers inward and back out several times while moving your hands upward. This indicates the flapping of wings.

FIGURE 13–9 *Butterfly*

Butterflies are beautiful but usually don't get too close to an active baby or toddler. If your baby does not get the chance to see one in person, find a variety of butterfly photographs in a book or on the Internet and use them to reinforce the sign.

WORM

The sign for WORM, as shown in **FIGURE 13–10**, depicts a worm curling itself up and down as it inches its way along.

1. **Hold your left forearm horizontally in front of your body.**
2. **Bend your right index finger to indicate the worm, and let it inch its way down the length of your arm.**

If your baby has never seen a worm up close, this is a good time to introduce them to her. Go outside and dig a couple of inches down in damp soil. Chances are excellent that you will discover a worm or two. Your child may be too excited by the discovery to focus on your sign, but keep modeling it anyway, as you never know when she may be taking it all in.

FIGURE 13–10 *Worm*

Chapter 14

Around the House Signs

Babies learning to speak will frequently dash through the house, pointing to objects and asking, "What's that?" Babies practicing sign will expect you to label each object with both the spoken word *and* its sign. The signs in this chapter represent common household items that a baby is likely to be interested in. Even when he inquires about an item for the hundredth time in a given day, try to answer each "What's that?" with a verbal and a signed label.

FURNITURE SIGNS

For babies and toddlers, furniture is something to climb on. Whether he recognizes other uses for these pieces of furniture or not, he may still want to know what each piece is. You will find other furniture signs in their related chapters. For example, the sign for BED can be found in Chapter 8, next to the sign for SLEEP. The sign for TABLE is located in Chapter 11 with other food-related signs.

CHAIR

The sign for CHAIR, as shown in **FIGURE 14–1**, uses both hands to illustrate the act of sitting.

1. Extend the index and middle fingers of your left hand horizontally in front of your body.
2. Curve the same fingers on your right hand and have them "sit" on your left fingers.
3. Lift your right fingers and have them sit again to complete the sign.

FIGURE 14–1 *Chair*

> ### E-FACT
>
> The sign for SIT is quite similar to CHAIR. In fact, they are identical except that SIT uses a single motion while CHAIR uses a double motion. So to indicate SIT, simply have your right fingers "sit" just once on your left hand.

Remember to use the sign for CHAIR for any kind of chair, not just the upholstered kind in your living room. Use it for dining room chairs, high chairs, lawn chairs, and rocking chairs. This will help your baby to understand that a chair is simply something to sit in and that the sign does not refer to one chair in particular.

COUCH

COUCH (**○ SEE DVD**) is a somewhat complicated sign, though it will be easier once you have learned the sign for CHAIR, or, more specifically, the sign for SIT.

1. Make the sign for SIT (as described in the preceding section).
2. Hold your hands like claws in front of you with your fingers pointed downward.
3. Move your hands several inches apart, to indicate the length of a couch. With this movement, you are showing a long place to sit.

SIGNS OF HOME

Of all the things in and on a home, doors and windows are probably among the most fascinating to a baby. Windows allow him to watch the ever-changing world outside, while doors actually provide a passageway to that world. When your child begins to demonstrate an interest in doors and windows, he will be ready to learn their corresponding signs.

DOOR

The sign for DOOR (**○ SEE DVD**) is formed like so.

1. Hold your arms vertically in front of your body and make the B hand shape with both hands, palms facing outward and index fingers touching.
2. Move your right hand a few inches away from your left hand, turning it while you do, so that your right hand is then perpendicular to your left.
3. Bring your right hand back to the original position to complete the sign.

In addition to outside doors, try using other doors to illustrate this sign to your baby. Cabinet doors, closet doors, and medicine-cabinet doors are all good to use. Just be sure to keep any hazardous chemicals and medicines out of your baby's reach.

E-ALERT

Depending on the complexity of the lock and the doorknob, a toddler may be able to open a door himself. A child who develops a sudden interest in going outside is especially likely to give it a try. Always keep doors well secured and do not leave your baby unattended, particularly in a room with an exterior door.

WINDOW

The sign for WINDOW (**O SEE DVD**) is similar to the sign for DOOR.

1. Hold your arms horizontally in front of your body and make the B hand shape with both hands, palms inward.
2. Rest the pinky finger of one hand on the index finger of the lower hand.
3. Raise the hand that is resting on top of the other a few inches and lower it down again.

KITCHEN SIGNS

Is the kitchen a playground for your baby? If so, you are in good company. Babies love to bang on pots and pans, pound on appliances, and splash in the sink. It's just plain fun. For this reason, the signs in this section should be particularly appealing to your child.

REFRIGERATOR

There are a few accepted versions of the sign for REFRIGERA-TOR. The one that will be easiest for your baby is shown in **FIGURE 14–2**; it simply simulates opening of a refrigerator door.

1. Hold your left hand up, palm facing toward the right.
2. Form your right hand into a fist, as if holding a refrigerator door handle.
3. Bring your fist toward your left palm.
4. Pull your fist away from the palm as if opening the refrigerator.

You can also follow up this sign by using the sign for COLD (see Chapter 17).

> ## E-SSENTIAL
>
> Babies, once they figure out how, love to open the refrigerator door. Perhaps it is the cold air rushing at them or just the opportunity to see what is inside that attracts them to this kitchen appliance. Use the opportunity to introduce your child not only to the sign for REFRIGERATOR, but also to the sign for OPEN.

SINK

SINK (**● SEE DVD**) is a three-part sign. Due to its complexity, you may want to wait until your child is an older toddler before introducing it.

1. Form the sign for WATER, which is made by tapping the W hand shape to your chin. (See page 125.)
2. Form the 3 hand shape (thumb, index finger, and middle finger extended) with both hands and use those fingers to turn two imaginary knobs twice.
3. Form the sign for BOWL, made by cupping both hands in front of your body and then bringing them up in the outline of a bowl.

FIGURE 14–2　*Refrigerator (Step One)*

FIGURE 14–2　*Refrigerator (Step Two)*

NOISY SIGNS

Noises around the house can be fun, but they can also be scary. Children (and adults, too) are usually most afraid of the things they do not understand. Introducing your baby to these signs will help him to understand what the sounds are. If your child does not startle easily, however, he may be excited by these noise-makers. If so, he should be eager to learn the signs for them.

TELEPHONE

The sign for TELEPHONE, as shown in **FIGURE 14–3**, is probably what you would expect it to be.

1. **Form the Y hand shape by extending your thumb and pinky finger.**
2. **Bring your hand up to the side of your face and touch your thumb to your ear and your pinky to your mouth.**

A fun way to help your child understand this sign is to give him a phone to play with. This can be a toy phone, a cellular phone that is no longer activated, or a home phone with the cord removed. In addition to using this playtime to reinforce the sign, try holding phone conversations with your child. He will likely find this amusing and want to do it again and again.

FIGURE 14–3 *Telephone*

TELEVISION

The easiest way to sign TELEVISION (**❍ SEE DVD**) is to spell it out with the T and V hand shapes.

1. **The T hand shape is formed by making a fist and extending your thumb up between your first and middle fingers.**
2. **The V hand shape is made by holding your first and middle fingers in a V.**

Another American Sign Language sign for TELEVISION requires outlining the shape of a box with your index fingers and then forming the letter V with your first and middle fingers. You then flick the letter V forward twice. Because this version of the sign is a bit more complex, you will probably find that your child is better able to form the first one.

E-ALERT

The American Academy of Pediatrics suggests that children age two years and younger abstain from watching television entirely. They further suggest that children over two not watch more than two hours of television per day, and that that should be limited to education and age-appropriate programming.

VACUUM CLEANER

To form the sign for VACUUM CLEANER (**SEE DVD**), simply pretend that you are vacuuming the floor.

1. Curl your fingers and extend your thumb as if holding the handle of a vacuum cleaner.
2. Push your hand back and forth as if vacuuming.

Is your baby afraid of the vacuum cleaner? Many babies are. Help your child to overcome his fear by allowing him to "vacuum." With the power turned off and the cord safely tucked away, allow your child to help you push the vacuum cleaner. If he is tall enough and willing, he can push it himself. This may help him to realize that the machine is not going to hurt him.

SIGNS OF THE TIME

A baby has absolutely no concept of time. But he is likely to notice the clock on the wall or on the bedside table. He may even be aware of the insistent ticking of an analog clock, and he will certainly notice a wake-up alarm. Whether it is the sight or the sound of a clock that piques his interest, he will certainly want to know what to call it.

If you have an analog clock with a plastic cover, allow your baby to hold it so that he can watch the second hand as it ticks by. The plastic cover is a necessity. Otherwise, your child would probably tug at the clock's hands, bending or even breaking them. This very basic household item can actually provide a great deal of entertainment for your little one.

E-SSENTIAL

A chiming clock can provide an easy counting lesson. Count each chime out loud as it sounds. When the chimes have finished, tell your baby the time. For instance, you might say, "It is ten o'clock. It's time to go outside." You can do this throughout the day for the parts of baby's routine that are scheduled.

FIGURE 14–4   *Clock (Step One)*

FIGURE 14–5   *Clock (Step Two)*

CLOCK

The sign for CLOCK, as shown in **FIGURES 14–4 AND 14–5**, is a two-step process.

1. Touch your wrist with a slightly curled index finger.
2. Form an open circle in the air with both hands, to indicate the shape of a wall clock.

This sign can be used with any clock. However, because a baby will not understand the function of a clock, he may be confused if you label two completely different objects with the same name and the same sign.

WATCH

The sign for WATCH (**⊙ SEE DVD**) starts out in the same way as the sign for CLOCK.

1. **Touch the top of your wrist with your slightly curled index finger.**
2. **Wrap your thumb and middle finger around your wrist, to indicate the band of a watch.**

Your child, of course, will probably start by wrapping all of his fingers around his wrist.

Babies are often interested in watches, primarily because they are something to play with. If you have an old plastic watch, see if your baby wants to wear it. You might find, however, that he is annoyed at having something attached to his wrist. If so, he will probably be content to clutch it in his hand. Just be sure that there are no loose pieces on the watch and that your baby is under close supervision while he plays with it. Alternatively, you could get him a toy watch that is intended for very young children.

OTHER HOUSEHOLD SIGNS

Of the hundreds or thousands of items found in a typical house, there are some things that babies seem to universally focus on. For example, is there a baby anywhere who is not enchanted by the steady whirl of a ceiling fan? And don't all babies adore playing with Mommy or Daddy's keys? In this section, you will find the signs for fans, keys, and all those other objects that so readily captivate a baby.

COMPUTER

There are several accepted signs for computer. The one shown in **FIGURE 14-6** is widely used and is probably easy enough for your child to learn.

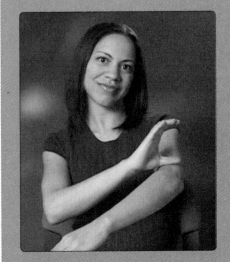

FIGURE 14-6 *Computer*

1. Hold your left arm horizontally in front of your body.
2. Form the letter C with your right hand.
3. Move the C up the length of your arm from your wrist to your elbow with a slight hopping motion.

> **E-ALERT**
>
> Although you may think of a computer as one unit with several components (CPU, monitor, keyboard, and mouse), your baby will see each of these things as individual entities. If you want your child to use the sign for each piece, wait until he is older to avoid overloading him with signs he can rarely use.

Because of the relative complexity of the sign for COMPUTER, watch out for your baby's attempts at this sign. He may run his fist up and down the length of his arm, or it may appear that he is simply rubbing his arm. Look for context clues to help you to determine what, if any, sign he is forming.

FAN

Most American Sign Language users are likely to simply spell out the word "fan" using the manual alphabet. There is another acceptable way to make this sign (**● SEE DVD**), and it will be much easier for your baby to learn.

1. Hold your hand in front of you, palm facing in.
2. Move your hand up and down, fanning yourself with your hand.

One way to help your baby make the connection between the object and the sign is to first hold your baby close enough to the fan so that he feels the air blowing. Then fan him with your hand, so that he also feels the air blowing. This will help him to understand the concept of the fan and how the sign relates to it.

KEYS

The sign for KEYS (**⊙ SEE DVD**) represents a key turning in a lock.

1. **Curl the index finger of your right hand into a tight hook.**
2. **Twist the hooked finger against the open palm of your left hand.**

E-FACT

There are toy keys on the market for every age and stage of a child's development. Many even come equipped with a toy version of a remote keyless entry device. If you find that your child is fascinated by your keys and can't seem to keep his hands off of them, consider getting him a set of his own.

Because "key" is such a simple word, some babies may begin saying it before they begin signing it. At that point, they will have little motivation to learn the sign. You might want to skip introducing signs for things your baby can say and you can understand. So if your baby can say "key," you might choose not to sign it with him. If you want your baby to continue signing into childhood, however, you can introduce the sign now or wait until he is a bit older and more interested in learning the sign.

LIGHT

There are a few different ways to sign LIGHT. Your baby will probably most often be referring to overhead lights when he signs LIGHT. Fortunately, this version, as shown in **FIGURES 14–7 AND 14–8**, is one of the easiest versions to form.

1. **Hold your hand up in the air near your head with your fingertips and thumb touching and pointed downward.**
2. **Open your hand up wide as if indicating a flash.**

FIGURE 14–7 *Light (Step One)*

FIGURE 14–8 *Light (Step Two)*

FIGURE 14–9 *Picture (Step One)*

FIGURE 14–10 *Picture (Step Two)*

PICTURE

The sign for PICTURE, as shown in **FIGURES 14–9 AND 14–10**, is meant to depict the transferring of the image of your face to film or a piece of paper.

1. Form the C hand shape with your right hand.
2. Meanwhile, hold your left hand up, palm facing to the right.
3. Bring the C up to your face and hold it there, slightly below your eye.
4. Bring it down and touch it to your open palm.

To help your child grasp the meaning of the sign, demonstrate it while exposing him to different types of pictures, including photographs and paintings.

Chapter 15

Signs of the Great Outdoors

From swings to flowers, snow to sunshine, there is so much for a baby to see outside. The world is constantly changing, and young children are stimulated by this ever-evolving environment. The more time your child spends outside, the more preferences she will develop for how her outdoor time is spent. There may be particular things she wants to play with or specific sights she wants to see. The signs in this chapter will enable her to let you know exactly what she wants to do when she goes outside.

SIGNS OF FUN

When your baby is old enough to enjoy the playground, she will likely make a beeline for the swings and the sandbox. You can use her interest in these things to your advantage when you introduce their signs. Keep in mind, however, that a playground can be a stimulating place with lots of things for your baby to see, hear, and do. If you can't seem to capture her attention for long enough to demonstrate these signs, just keep trying and waiting for an opportunity.

SAND

SAND, as shown in **FIGURE 15–1**, is an early favorite for many young children, and it's easy to sign, too!

1. Open your hand in front of you, palm facing upward.
2. Use the fingers of the opposite hand as though you are sprinkling sand on top of your open palm.

SWING

Swings are fun for people of all ages. Your baby likely got her first taste of a swing while she was still a very young infant. It may take a while for your baby to master SWING (**⊙ SEE DVD**). In the meantime, you may find that she simply links her hands together and swings them back and forth.

1. Extend the first and middle fingers of your left hand horizontally in front of your body. This represents the seat of the swing.
2. Take the same fingers of your right hand, and hook them over the left fingers. This represents legs dangling from the swing.
3. With your fingers hooked together, swing both hands back and forth twice.

FIGURE 15–1 *Sand*

E-ALERT

Swings can be hazardous to a baby or toddler. Be sure to keep your child out of the way of a moving swing, and only allow her to ride on a swing specifically designed for young children or babies. A regular swing does not provide enough support to keep a little one from falling out.

SIGNS OF LIFE

While your baby doesn't yet understand that plants are living things that change and grow, she is probably awed by their distinct attributes, such as the impressive height of the trees and the bold colors of the flowers. Use her awe to your advantage. When you see her gazing up at a tree, or attempting to pluck a flower, model the corresponding sign for her. You can also use these signing opportunities to incorporate lessons about nature, colors, and many other things that relate to plant growth.

FLOWER

The sign FLOWER (**◉ SEE DVD**) displays the correlation between flower and nose.

1. Draw the tips of all of your fingers and thumb together as if operating a hand puppet with its mouth closed, as you did with the sign for EAT (page 79).
2. Touch the tips of those fingers first to one side of your nose and then to the other.

When you first introduce this sign, try to expose your child to as many types of flowers as possible. This will prevent her from understanding the sign to mean one specific type of flower. And be sure to let her see you sniffing the flower. Let her know how good it smells, and hold it up to her nose. This will help her to see a correlation between the flower and her nose. That, in turn, will help to reinforce the sign.

GRASS

The sign for GRASS can be confusing. Check carefully (**○ SEE DVD**) to see the sign demonstrated.

1. Touch your open palm to the underside of your chin.
2. Pull your hand out and away from your face. Your hand should not go straight out, however, but rather make a slight arc.
3. Bring your palm back to your chin and repeat the motion.

> **E-FACT**
>
> In 2005, 7.7 million children in the U.S. were reported to suffer from hay fever, an allergy caused by exposure to grass and other pollens. If your child is afflicted, keep her indoors during the morning hours when pollen is at its worst, and keep your grass cut short.

At first, your baby may only see the grass as ground covering and may not have any interest in signing it. But as you and she spend more time playing in the grass, she will begin to take notice of it, and you may notice her examining the blades and picking it, like a flower.

TREE

The sign for TREE, as shown in **FIGURE 15–2**, is fun to form and is a great representation of an actual tree.

1. Hold your left arm in front of your body, palm downward.
2. Rest the elbow of your right arm on the back of your left hand. The fingers of your right hand should be extended.
3. Twist the right hand a few times.

FIGURE 15–2 *Tree*

SIGNS FOR MAN-MADE SIGHTS

Humans have left their mark in the great outdoors. Even in your own front yard, your baby will be exposed to these man-made sights, and she will likely be curious about many of them. She will particularly want to know about her own home. It is a structure that she sees every day, and she will probably want a label for it. Give her one with both a word and a sign. Soon, she will be signing it on her own.

HOUSE

The sign for HOUSE, as shown in **FIGURES 15–3 AND 15–4**, is simple to form. You trace the outline of a house in the air.

1. **Raise both your arms in front of you and form the top of a triangle by touching your fingertips together. This depicts the roof of a house.**
2. **Bring your hands down, outlining the shape of a box. This depicts the sides of a house.**

Help your baby by using it in reference to many different houses. Point out houses of different sizes, shapes, and colors so that she has a good representation of what a house is.

HOME

While HOUSE refers to any building where people dwell, HOME (**○ SEE DVD**) refers to the specific structure where baby lives.

1. **Draw the tips of all of your fingers and your thumb together, as if operating a hand puppet with its mouth closed.**
2. **Touch your hand to your lips.**
3. **Bring your fingertips up to your cheek, near your ear.**

FIGURE 15–3 *House (Step One)*

FIGURE 15–4 *House (Step Two)*

Consistency is the key to using this sign. Every time you arrive home, either on foot or in the car, take a moment to show your baby the sign for HOME. Always demonstrate excitement when forming this sign so that your baby understands that home is a happy place.

STREET

The sign for STREET (**◉ SEE DVD**) may very well remind you of the sign for PANTS (page 93).

1. **Hold your hands several inches apart in front of your body, with palms facing each other.**
2. **Move your hands outward as if outlining a road or path.**

E-SSENTIAL

No matter how young your child, it is never too early to teach her to look both ways before crossing the street. Any time you cross the street with your child, stop and look both ways, and narrate your actions. This will instill the habit in your child at an early age.

As you show this sign to your child, be sure to emphasize to her that the street is for cars to drive on, and model the sign for CAR. This gives you the opportunity to work on the signs for CAR and STREET simultaneously, and it is also a good reminder for your child that the street is not a place to play.

SIGNS IN THE SKY

The sky is full of spectacular things for your baby to see. Demonstrating the signs for these things can also provide you with numerous opportunities for quality time. For example, spend some time on a beautiful sunny day lying in the grass and watching the clouds go by. Or, on a warm rainy day, take your child outside to jump in the puddles. For a nighttime excursion, point out the stars and the moon to your baby. All of these will give your child a learning experience as well as bonding time with you.

CLOUD

The sign for CLOUD (**FIGURE 15–5**) is formed by making fluffy cloud shapes with your hands.

1. **Spread both hands open.**
2. **Hold one hand palm up and the other hand hovering over it palm down.**
3. **Slowly move both hands to the side, making arcs as you go to indicate the fluffiness of clouds.**

E-FACT

Clouds will be easiest for your child to spot when they are stark white against a vibrant blue sky. If it is overcast or gray, it will be harder for your child to discern the clouds from the sky, and she may not understand what you are trying to point out to her.

MOON

To remember the sign for MOON (**⊙ SEE DVD**) just think of your eye looking toward the moon at night.

1. **Curve the thumb and first finger of your right hand into a crescent shape and hold it up to your face.**
2. **Pull your hand up and away from your face a few inches.**

FIGURE 15–5   *Cloud*

RAIN

RAIN is a fairly straightforward sign and might be just what you would expect.

1. Hold your hands up with your fingers extended, as shown in **FIGURE 15–6.**
2. Bring your hands down to indicate raindrops falling.
3. Repeat the motion to complete the sign.

FIGURE 15–6 *Rain*

> ### E-ALERT
>
> Once your baby experiences rain up close, you may find that she uses the sign for WATER to indicate rain. This means that your baby is using logic and reasoning to identify the things around her. Be sure to praise her efforts, even if you continue to reinforce the sign for RAIN.

The next time a rainy day keeps you and your baby indoors, use the sign in a song as you watch the rain fall. There are plenty of children's rain-related songs you can use, including "The Itsy Bitsy Spider," "Rain Rain Go Away," and "It's Raining, It's Pouring."

SNOW

Once you've learned the sign for RAIN, the sign for SNOW (**⊙ SEE DVD**) is very simple to master.

1. As with RAIN, hold your hands up with your fingers extended.
2. As you bring your hands down, however, flutter your fingers to represent the lightness of snowflakes falling.

Playing in the snow is a very sensory experience. Not only is the snow beautiful to look at, it is also interesting to touch, taste, and hear. Let your child feel how cold the snow is with her hand. Ask her to listen to the sound of crunching footsteps. Set out a clean container to collect the snow and let her taste it. These experiences will be educational for her and fun for you both.

STAR

Think of the sign for STAR as representing a shooting star.

1. Extend your index fingers and touch them together, as shown in **FIGURE 15–7**.
2. Raise one finger several inches above the other, as shown in **FIGURE 15–8**.
3. Raise the other finger above the first.
4. Repeat, alternating fingers.

SUN

The sign for SUN (**⊙ SEE DVD**) is the same as the sign for LIGHT as demonstrated in Chapter 14.

1. Hold your hand slightly above your head, fingertips pressed together and facing toward your head.
2. Open your fingers wide as if indicating a flash.

FIGURE 15–7 *Star (Step One)*

FIGURE 15–8 *Star (Step Two)*

THUNDER

The sign for THUNDER (**◉ SEE DVD**) is a two-motion sign.

1. Touch your ear with your index finger to indicate something is being heard.
2. Shake both fists in the air to represent a vibrating noise.

As the second motion will probably be the most fascinating of the two to your child, you may find that he forgets the first part altogether.

> ### E-FACT
>
> You can calculate how far you are from a lightning strike by counting the seconds that pass between a flash of lightning and a rumble of thunder. Divide the number of seconds by five and you will get the number of miles between you and the lightning. This can be a helpful calculation to ease a child who is frightened by the thunder.

Thunder can be a frightening noise for a young child. To combat this problem, try being silly while demonstrating the sign. Make funny (but happy) faces and exaggerate the shaking of the fists. When your baby signs in return, react with glee. This will help your child to equate the sound of thunder with something fun.

SIGNS OF WATER

If you are lucky enough to live on the water, you will have many opportunities to use the signs in this section. Even if you don't, your baby can still use these signs during a weekend visit to the lake or the beach or when she sees these bodies of water in books or on television. Keep in mind, however, that it is common for babies to use the sign for WATER to refer to any body of water, from bathtubs to oceans.

LAKE

The sign for LAKE (● **SEE DVD**) is somewhat complex and may take a bit of practice for you and your baby to learn.

1. Tap the W hand shape to your chin, making the sign for WATER.
2. Hold both hands in front of your body with your index fingers and thumbs forming a large open circle.
3. With your fingers still extended, bring your hands together as you would for the sign for PLATE.

OCEAN

The sign for OCEAN (● **SEE DVD**) is made by forming waves with your hands.

1. Tap the W hand shape to your chin, making the sign for WATER.
2. With the palm of your hand facing down, move your hand away from your face, as if climbing a hill, and then back down again.
3. Repeat this motion a few times to complete the sign.

Will your child actually be able to tell the difference between a lake and an ocean? It depends on her age, the size of the lake, and how much exposure she has to each body of water. Just don't be surprised to find that she uses one sign for all bodies of water.

Chapter 16

Transportation Signs

Planes, trains, and automobiles—whether it is because of the sounds they make or the way they move, babies are captivated by them. They love to gaze at, point to, and babble about these massive machines from the time they are alert enough to notice them. Encourage your baby's interest by showing him the signs for these vehicles. He will be eager to learn them, and you will both enjoy signing them.

SIGNS OF FLYING

Your baby will have no understanding of the function of an aircraft, but you can be sure that he notices every time one soars through the sky above him. If he shows a particularly strong interest in aircraft, try taking him to an airport to see airplanes and possibly helicopters up close. Commercial airports have numerous restrictions that make it nearly impossible to get too close to an airplane, but some smaller airports will allow you to walk around on the tarmac and look at the parked planes.

AIRPLANE

The sign for AIRPLANE (❍ **SEE DVD**) is made with the same hand formation as the sign for I LOVE YOU.

1. **Extend your index finger, pinky, and thumb of your right hand.**
2. **Make a jabbing motion in the air and then bring your hand up and over your head in an arc.**

You can often hear an airplane before it is visible in the sky. This gives you a great opportunity to demonstrate the sign before your baby is too busy watching the plane to notice. As soon as you hear it, ask your baby if *he* hears the airplane. As you say it, form the sign in his line of sight. Soon the plane will be visible, and he will make the connection.

HELICOPTER

HELICOPTER takes a bit of practice to form.

1. **Extend the index finger, middle finger, and thumb of your left hand with your thumb pointed upward, as shown in FIGURE 16–1.**
2. **Place the palm of your right hand onto the thumb of your left.**
3. **Shake your right hand in a rolling motion to represent the helicopter's blades.**

FIGURE 16–1 *Helicopter*

Initially, your baby might have some trouble differentiating between an airplane and a helicopter. In time, as he works harder to pay attention to these flying machines, he will pick up on their differences. As you continue to model each sign, this will help to reinforce the fact that helicopters and airplanes are two entirely different things.

E-FACT

The first manned helicopter flight took place in 1907 in an early version of the aircraft called the Gyroplane No. 1. This first flight lasted one minute and took the helicopter and its pilot about two feet into the air. It was 1936 before any viable helicopters took to the skies.

SIGNS ON THE ROAD

Vehicles on the road are a far more frequent sighting than vehicles in the sky. Because of this repeated exposure, your baby will probably learn these signs rather quickly. But don't just wait for an automobile to pass by. Demonstrate these signs while you are stopped at red lights, riding a bus, or when you are a passenger in a car.

CAR

CAR may be one of the easiest signs you and your baby will learn.

1. Hold your hands in front of you as if holding on to a steering wheel, as shown in **FIGURE 16–2**.
2. Move your hands up and down as if steering the wheel.

In the beginning, your baby may use the sign for CAR to describe everything on wheels. If it is important to you that he

FIGURE 16–2 *Car*

uses the correct sign, just keep modeling it, but acknowledge his efforts. For example, if a truck drives by and your baby signs CAR, you could say, "You're right, that does look like a car. It is a truck and it is bigger than a car."

E-SSENTIAL

In most states, children are required to ride in a forward-facing car seat from the time they are one year old until they are four or five years old. After that, many states require children to ride in a booster seat until they are six, seven, or even eight years of age.

BUS

The sign for BUS (**◉ SEE DVD**) is simply spelled out using the American Sign Language manual alphabet. The complete manual alphabet can be found in Appendix C of this book. Because of the dexterity that finger spelling requires, your baby will almost certainly be unable to form this sign until he is older. If you wish to introduce it to him now, consider creating your own sign to indicate BUS. If you do choose to make up your own sign, try demonstrating it while singing "The Wheels on the Bus." This fun song offers many opportunities for signing, and children usually love it.

MOTORCYCLE

The sign for MOTORCYCLE (**◉ SEE DVD**) is a fun one that your child will probably enjoy forming.

1. **Hold your hands in front of you, curled up into fists, as if holding onto the handlebars of a motorcycle.**
2. **Twist your hands forward twice to indicate revving up the engine.**

At first, your child may twist both hands when making the sign. Likewise, he may curl his hands into fists but neglect to twist either of them.

E-ALERT

Sometimes a child who is interested in motorcycles is afraid of them up close. The loudness of the bike's engine is probably the culprit. If your child is curious but afraid to get too close, hold him at a safe distance and then point out the various parts of the bike.

Don't be surprised if your baby begins to form this sign every time he hears a loud engine, whether it belongs to a motorcycle or not. The distinct sound of a motorcycle is the way that some babies identify them. If you see that the engine does not belong to a motorcycle, praise your child anyway. Tell him that he is right, the car (or truck or lawn mower) *does* sound like a motorcycle. Then explain to him the differences in the vehicles. He may not understand your explanation, but it gives you an opportunity to converse with him, something that should be done frequently.

TRUCK

The sign for TRUCK is almost identical to the sign for CAR, as you can see in **FIGURE 16–3**.

1. Hold your hands in front of you as if holding on to a steering wheel. The difference between this sign and the sign for CAR is that your hands are spread wider, as if holding the large steering wheel of a truck.
2. Move your hands side to side as if moving the wheel.

Because of the subtle difference between the two signs, your baby may appear to use the same sign to mean both

FIGURE 16–3 *Truck*

"car" and "truck." Just be sure to label the vehicles verbally as well to help your baby learn the proper names.

WATER TRAVEL SIGNS

Even if your baby's only water time is in the bathtub, he will still have ample opportunity to use the signs in this section. After all, toy boats are a bath-time staple, and nearly all young children like to "swim" in the tub. If your baby does get the opportunity to visit bodies of water such as pools, lakes, or even the ocean, he will have even more opportunity to use these signs.

BOAT

The sign for BOAT, as shown in **FIGURE 16–4**, is simple to form.

1. **Cup your hands in the shape of a boat.**
2. **Bob your "boat" up and down slightly as if it were on the water.**

> **E-FACT**
>
> There are different signs for different types of boats. Sailboats have one sign, while cruise ships have another and canoes another still. Your baby will be unlikely to differentiate between water craft, so using a single sign for every boat is sufficient until your child is older and better able to notice a difference.

FIGURE 16–4 *Boat*

A great time to demonstrate this sign is while your child is taking a bath. Give him a toy boat to play with, and then form the sign for BOAT with your hands. Then put your hands into the water and have them "float" next to the boat to help your child connect the sign with the object it represents.

SWIM

SWIM (**○ SEE DVD**) is signed by pretending to do the breast stroke.

1. Hold both hands in front of your body.
2. Push your hands, palms outward, to the side, as if swimming.
3. Repeat the motion to complete the sign.

Unless your child takes swimming lessons or spends a lot of time at the pool, he may not have too many opportunities to use this sign. If he doesn't need it, there is no sense in introducing him to signs that he will not be able to use.

PEDAL POWER SIGNS

Chances are that when your child is old enough to ride a tricycle, he will be old enough to speak the word. In the meantime, he may use the sign to point out these two- and three-wheeled contraptions when they pass by on the street. If your child has older siblings who ride bikes, he will be probably be even more interested in them.

BICYCLE

The sign for BICYCLE, as shown in **FIGURE 16–5**, resembles feet pedaling.

1. Hold both hands in front of your body and make them into fists.
2. Rotate each hand in a forward circle, as if pedaling with them.

Some babies may be more interested in the person riding the bicycle than the bicycle itself. If this is the case with your baby, point out bicycles without riders, such as those on a bicycle rack or in a store. Some babies may even confuse a bike for a car when they notice the wheels.

FIGURE 16–5 *Bicycle*

TRICYCLE

TRICYCLE starts out with the sign for bicycle.

1. Hold both hands in front of your body and make them into fists.
2. Rotate each hand in a forward circle, as if pedaling with them.
3. After pedaling with your fists indicate the three wheels by holding up three fingers (thumb, index finger, and middle finger), as shown in **FIGURE 16–6**.

FIGURE 16–6 *Tricycle*

E-ALERT

The sign for TRICYCLE is not one that is widely used in the Deaf community and may not be readily understood by everyone. However, you are in good company because many other parents who are using American Sign Language with their babies also use this sign.

This sign is quite complicated, and your baby will probably have some difficulty with it. You may find that it is easier, though not entirely accurate, to use BICYCLE to describe both a bike and a tricycle. You could also consider making up your own sign for the three-wheeled vehicle.

SIGNS OF POUNDING THE PAVEMENT

Does your baby love to go for walks? Does he pull on your hand to lead you down the street or try to climb into the stroller? If so, your baby is going to love the signs in this section. They will give him all the communication tools he needs to let you know he wants to go for a stroll. These signs may also be easy for your baby to acquire because you will have numerous opportunities throughout the day to demonstrate them.

RUN

Obviously, you and your child won't be able to demonstrate the sign for RUN while he is running. Instead, model the sign, as shown in **FIGURE 16–7**, when you see other children running.

1. Hold both hands in front of the body with index fingers extended and thumbs upward.
2. Hook the index finger of your right hand with the thumb of your left hand.
3. Move the entire formation forward while wiggling the index finger of your left hand and the thumb of your right.

STROLLER

STROLLER (**◯ SEE DVD**) is an easy sign to form, but as it is difficult to model this sign while your child is riding in the stroller, be on the lookout for other parents pushing strollers. Your baby will probably take notice of them, and that will provide you with an ideal moment to model the sign.

1. Hold your fists in front of your body as if holding onto the handlebars of a stroller.
2. Push your fists forward to complete the sign.

FIGURE 16–7 *Run*

> ### E-SSENTIAL
>
> Even the youngest toddlers love to push a toy stroller around. It gives them a chance to imitate their mother or father and the opportunity to wheel something around, much like a car. Giving your toddler a toy stroller is also a great way to teach him about caring for a baby, if he has a sibling on the way.

WALK

To form the sign for WALK, just let your fingers do the walking, as shown in **FIGURE 16–8**.

1. **Hold your hand out in front of your body and extend the index and middle fingers, curling the remaining fingers into your palm.**
2. **Point your extended fingers downward.**
3. **Move your extended fingers back and forth as if they were legs walking.**

The best time to demonstrate this sign is actually not while taking a walk with your child. There are far too many things to see for your baby to pay much attention to your signing efforts. Instead, ask your baby if he would like to take a walk, and then demonstrate the sign. Be sure that his shoes and jacket are already on because you will want to take him outside immediately and go for the walk to help him associate the sign with the action.

FIGURE 16–8 *Walk*

TRAIN

The sign for TRAIN (**O SEE DVD**) is a fun sign for baby to demonstrate because it depicts a train on tracks.

1. **Extend the first and middle fingers of your left hand and hold them in front of your body.**
2. **Extend the first and middle fingers of your right hand and lay them perpendicularly over the left fingers.**
3. **Move the right fingers up and down the length of the left ones to represent a train on tracks.**

A great time to introduce this sign is when stopped by a train in the car. You and your baby can both pass the time by practicing the sign. Depending on his signing abilities, he may even be able to acquire the sign during one stop at the railroad tracks.

Chapter 17

Signs for Concepts

It can be difficult for babies and young toddlers to grasp the meaning of intangible things such as concepts and ideas. When your baby does develop an understanding of such concepts, the signs in this chapter will help her to express them long before she can ever verbalize them. Ironically, many of these concepts that can be so difficult to understand have corresponding signs that will be extremely simple for your child to form.

SIGNS OF SIZE

It is very simple to illustrate the concepts of big and small to your child. Take two similar objects of different sizes and present them to your baby. For instance, show your child one small pink ball and one large pink ball, or one small square block and one large square block. These items should be similar enough that their difference in size is what stands out. It is also preferable to use an object that your baby is already familiar with so that you aren't trying to demonstrate the name of the object and the difference in size at the same time.

To introduce the signs, offer her one of the objects and say, for instance, "See the big pink ball." While you are doing so, be sure to sign BIG and even BALL if that is a sign you have already taught. Then hand her the other ball and say, "See the small pink ball." Next, try the same exercise with two other big and small objects so that your baby understands that it does not apply only to balls or any other single item.

BIG

Although this sign for BIG (◉ **SEE DVD**) is American Sign Language, it is almost identical to a baby's natural gesture for "big."

1. **Hold your hands a few inches apart in front of your body with palms facing each other.**
2. **Spread your hands apart just beyond the width of your body to illustrate the size of an object.**

When you first begin to demonstrate this sign, be sure to use objects with obvious size differences. A baby may not pick up on a subtle difference, and this could lead to confusion. One good way to show an obvious size difference is by showing your baby a toy or model version of the object and then the real-life object, such as a toy car and a real car.

E-ALERT

Do not be surprised if your baby is eighteen months of age or older before she begins to understand concepts such as space, size, and dimension. Don't feel like you have to wait to introduce the signs, however. Using them now will help her to learn and understand the concepts.

SMALL

The sign for SMALL (**⊙ SEE DVD**) is just the opposite of the sign for BIG.

1. **Start with your hands in front of your body several inches apart, palms facing each other.**
2. **Bring them together so that they are just a couple of inches apart.**

In the beginning, you may find that your baby claps her hands when she brings them together. If she does, be sure to praise her efforts, and make a mental note to look for something small if she makes a single clap in the future.

SIGNS FOR BABY'S FIRST PREPOSITIONS

Do you remember taking English in junior high school and having to memorize a list of dozens of prepositions? Some teachers even turned those prepositions into a song: "About, above across, after, against . . ." Fortunately for your baby, she has several years before she will be required to memorize them all. In the meantime, there are a few that she will find useful in her everyday life, even as a young child.

Although these prepositions represent intangible concepts, they will not be as difficult as some for your child to understand. She undoubtedly experiences these concepts in her everyday life and will therefore have some understanding of them. Additionally, this means that there will be numerous opportunities to demonstrate these signs to her.

E-FACT

If it has been a while since you took grammar in school, prepositions are words or phrases that show the relationship between a noun and another word. For example, in the sentence, "The spoon is under the chair," *under* is the preposition that shows the relationship of the spoon to the chair.

IN

The sign for IN, as shown in **FIGURE 17–1**, is formed by inserting one hand into the other.

1. **Hold one hand in front of your body, palm facing toward you.**
2. **Bring your other hand up, and with fingers together, insert it into the palm of the first hand.**

This sign will be especially useful to your baby when she begins filling up containers for fun. Babies love to fill boxes, buckets, and bins with almost any object that will fit inside. Use this to your advantage, and instruct your child to put her toys in her toy box.

Another good way to demonstrate this sign is by using it when going indoors after playing outside. Announce to your child that it is time to go in, putting emphasis on the word "in" and signing it simultaneously. Then immediately take her inside.

FIGURE 17–1 *In*

OUT

The sign for OUT (**⊙ SEE DVD**) is the opposite of the sign for IN.

1. **Start with one hand enclosed in the other, as described in the previous section for the sign for IN.**
2. **Pull your fingers out of the palm and separate your hands from each other.**

In the same way that babies love to fill containers, they also (and perhaps even more so) love to empty them. Each time she pulls the blocks out of the block box or the socks out of your drawer, demonstrate the sign for OUT.

FIGURE 17–2   *Up (Step One)*

> ## E-SSENTIAL
>
> The word "out," by itself, is not actually a preposition. "Outside" is, however, and so is "out of." Your baby will not be concerned with the rules of grammar, though, and so due to the simplicity of her vocabulary, she will undoubtedly use OUT by itself to mean both "out of" and "outside."

In the same way that you might sign IN to tell your child that it is time to go inside, you can also use the sign for OUT to let her know it is time to go outside. When she is ready to go, simply tell her that it is time to go out, and form the sign.

UP

The sign for UP is about as simple as it gets.

1. **Point your index finger upward, as shown in FIGURE 17–2.**
2. **Raise your arm a few inches, as shown in FIGURE 17–3.**

When introducing this sign and this concept, be sure to use objects with which your baby is already very familiar. You

FIGURE 17–3   *Up (Step Two)*

don't want her to understand the sign for UP as the sign for that object. If she already knows the sign for BALL, have someone toss a ball up in the air while you demonstrate the sign. Be sure to tell her verbally that the ball is up.

DOWN

As easy as UP is, DOWN (**○ SEE DVD**) is just as simple.

1. **Point your index finger downward.**
2. **Lower your finger a few inches.**

Use the countless times that your baby drops something as opportunities to demonstrate the sign. For instance, when she drops her spoon from her high chair, don't rush to pick it up. Instead, wait until she peers over the side of her chair and spots it on the floor. Then form the sign for DOWN and tell her, "Uh-oh, your spoon fell down."

Another good way to demonstrate the sign is by taking your baby somewhere high up, with a view of just about anything. Such a place could include a balcony, the second story of a mall, or a scenic lookout. Point out things below and let her know that these things are down. For example, if you are looking down at a lower level of a shopping mall, you might point out a baby to your child and say, "See the baby down there?" while you form the sign for DOWN.

SIGNS OF GOOD MANNERS

Even very young toddlers are known to say "please" and "thank you." They seem to learn early on that using these magic words will help to get them what they want. If you wish to instill good manners in your child at an even earlier age, model the signs. These are good concept signs to introduce early because they are simple to form and are familiar in their meanings. Be patient with your baby, though, and remember that children of all ages occasionally need to be reminded to use their manners.

PLEASE

The sign for PLEASE is a simple one but is perhaps best demonstrated through example.

1.   **Place your hand flat against your chest, as shown in FIGURE 17–4.**
2.   **Move your hand around in a circular motion.**

The original intent of this sign was to express pleasure, as in "I am *pleased* to hear you say that." Now, though, the sign has gained widespread use in the Deaf community as a sign of politeness when making a request, as in, "Will you *please* do this for me?"

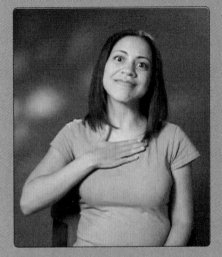

FIGURE 17–4 *Please*

E-FACT

Most children are unable to consistently say "please" and "thank you" until they are at least two years of age. So even once your child has learned the signs for these words, she may not use them every time. In the meantime, praise her when she does remember, and offer her a gentle reminder when she does not.

Even if the other members of your household don't sign with your baby, try to get them on board with this sign. If your baby sees others signing PLEASE when making their requests, she will begin to understand the connection between a request and the sign. Likewise, if you ask your baby to do something or hand you something, be sure to sign PLEASE to her, as well.

FIGURE 17–5 *Thank You (Step One)*

FIGURE 17–6 *Thank You (Step Two)*

THANK YOU

The sign for THANK YOU looks as if you are blowing a kiss.

1. **Bring the tips of your fingers to your lips, as shown in FIGURE 17–5.**
2. **Extend your palm out flat, as shown in FIGURE 17–6.**

There are plenty of opportunities to model this sign. Every time your child gives you something or does something helpful, exclaim, "Thank you!" and form the sign. Then try giving something back to her and look at her expectantly, as if waiting for her to do something. If she does not form the sign, simply demonstrate it for her again. It will take time, but she will eventually understand the concept.

BASIC TEMPERATURE SIGNS

It doesn't take long for a baby to figure out the difference between hot and cold. Of course, it is important to be careful when teaching your baby about heat. Fortunately, you do not have to expose her to anything that is overly hot to teach the concept. Instead, teach your baby by showing her the differences between warm and cold.

One good way to introduce hot and cold to your baby is by using the faucet. Turn the water on to warm. It should be quite warm, but not scalding. Allow your baby to touch the water and tell her that it is hot water. After she has tried this a few times, turn the water to cold. Have her put her hand back under the faucet and tell her that it is cold water. There are plenty of other ways to teach the concept, but the water method will be easy for you and your baby.

COLD

To form the sign for COLD, imagine that you are, in fact, cold.

1. **Draw your shoulders in and bring your forearms up to your chest with your hands balled into fists, as shown in FIGURE 17–7.**
2. **Shake your hands as if you are cold.**

Seek out opportunities to use this sign to help reinforce its meaning. For instance, if it's cold outside, use the sign when you step out the door. You could also let your baby play with an ice cube while you demonstrate the sign. You will find multiple opportunities in your everyday life to use this sign. This will help your baby to learn the sign and its meaning quickly.

FIGURE 17–7   *Cold*

HOT

The sign for HOT (**◉ SEE DVD**) is formed by starting with your fingertips at your lips, similar to the sign for EAT (page 79).

1. **Draw the tips of all of your fingers and thumb together as if operating a hand puppet with its mouth closed and bring them to your mouth, as in the sign for EAT.**
2. **Pull your fingers away and downward as if pulling something from your mouth that is too hot. Spread your fingers apart as you move your hand down.**

As with COLD, you will have plenty of chances to demonstrate the sign for HOT. If you put your baby in the car on a summer afternoon, be sure to tell her how hot it is. If her food is too hot to eat, let her know by forming the sign. It won't be long before she is telling you when something is too hot.

SIGNS FOR ALL GONE AND MORE

ALL GONE and MORE are concepts that babies learn at an early age, usually as they apply to food. In fact, these are among the first signs that many parents choose to introduce to their babies. ALL GONE is a great sign for parents to use to let their children know when there is no more of a given thing, such as a snack or a beverage. MORE is almost always used by a child to ask for more of what she wants. As your child becomes familiar with the signs, expect them both to get quite a bit of use.

ALL GONE

ALL GONE (● **SEE DVD**) is a very descriptive sign.

1. **Extend your hand, palm upward.**
2. **Blow across your palm, as if blowing something away.**

Every time your baby finishes eating or drinking, show her the empty container, say "all gone," and form the sign. The sign does not only have to apply to food, though. Whenever anything disappears from sight, you can use the sign. For example, if your child is watching an airplane fly across the sky, use the sign for ALL GONE when the plane is no longer visible. Your child will soon understand that the sign is used when something that was once there, is no more.

MORE

MORE is a favorite sign for babies and is an easy one to form.

1. **Hold both hands in front of you, fingers on each hand held together and thumbs tucked in.**
2. **Tap the fingertips of both hands together, as shown in FIGURE 17–8.**

FIGURE 17–8 *More*

To your baby, this sign may resemble the sign for BALL. Until she has the sign mastered, the context of the sign should clue you in to what she is really saying.

When preverbal babies want more of something, they usually whine, cry, grunt, or point in an effort to make their desires known. You are probably quite familiar with your baby's usual "sign" for more. To reinforce the American Sign Language sign for MORE, simply model it each time she asks for more of anything. On the other hand, if your child's current method for asking for more is acceptable to you, continue to use it. There is no reason to use signs with your child that she does not need.

DEFINITIVE SIGNS

These signs represent conclusive concepts with which your baby may already be familiar. Most children understand "yes" and "no" very early. Nonetheless, introducing the signs for these concepts will help to reinforce their meaning, as emphasis will be placed on the words and your baby will gain added exposure to them.

NO

The sign for NO (**SEE DVD**) is easy to form.

1. **Extend the thumb, index finger, and middle finger of your right hand.**
2. **Bring the fingertips together with the fingers flattened, almost as if trying to indicate someone talking.**

E-FACT

Most babies understand the word "no" by the time they are ten months old. This is undoubtedly due to the fact that curious babies who love to explore hear the word so often. In spite of this early understanding, babies will often choose to ignore it when it is directed at them.

Many babies shake their heads to indicate "no." If that gesture is working for you and your baby, you might want to skip this sign altogether. Otherwise, demonstrate the sign *while* shaking your head. This will help your baby to connect the word and the head shake with the corresponding sign.

YES

The sign for YES (**⊙ SEE DVD**) can be made in tandem with a nod of the head or by itself.

1. Make a fist with your right hand.
2. Flick it forward at the wrist, as if your hand is nodding.

Although a shake of the head for "no" is more common among young babies, many also nod their heads for "yes." If your baby is already nodding, you may find that you do not need the American Sign Language sign for YES. As with "no," if you wish to use the sign anyway, start by doing both signing and nodding. Nodding is a natural gesture anyway, and there is no need to drop it in order to use the sign.

OPEN

Obviously, a great way to demonstrate the sign for OPEN is by opening a door repeatedly and forming the sign.

1. Hold your hands in front of your body, palms down, index fingers touching, as shown in **FIGURE 17-9**.
2. Pull your hands apart, flipping them over as you do so, as shown in **FIGURE 17-10**, to demonstrate something opening.

There are, of course, other things to be opened besides doors. Open jars, boxes, cabinets, and books to help your child grasp the concept of opening something.

FIGURE 17-9 *Open (Step One)*

FIGURE 17-10 *Open (Step Two)*

SHUT

The sign for SHUT (**⊙ SEE DVD**) is just the opposite of the sign for OPEN.

1. Begin with your hands several inches apart with palms facing up.
2. Bring them around and together so that your index fingers are touching and your palms are facing downward.

Many toddlers find it amusing to shut the door. They especially love to close themselves in a room. If your baby does this, use the opportunity to introduce her to the sign for SHUT.

E-SSENTIAL

Although shutting a door can be great fun, it can also be problematic if a child locks herself into a room. Be sure that you remember to childproof the doors in your home by installing doorknob guards, safety locks, and even doorstops to prevent little fingers from getting jammed in a closing door.

As with OPEN, try to find ways other than doors to demonstrate the sign for SHUT. You can shut a lid, a window, or a drawer. Be forewarned, however, that your child may take great delight in shutting everything that happens to be left open.

Chapter 18

Signs of Feelings and Affection

As a parent, you have undoubtedly discovered that babies are affectionate and emotional creatures. They love to dole out hugs and kisses, and they are quick to display their feelings of both joy and sadness. All of the signs in this chapter will give your baby the tools he needs to communicate his feelings. This newfound communication will likely result in fewer temper tantrums for him and fewer frustrations for you.

SIGNS OF AFFECTION

Most babies and toddlers love hugs and kisses and most parents do, too. You may wonder, however, what purpose is served by introducing these signs. After all, a baby who wants a hug or a kiss will simply give it. These signs are most used by babies who are labeling the actions of others. For example, a baby may witness his family members hugging, and if he knows the sign for HUG, he can indicate it. In the same way that a baby learning to talk loves to label things with the spoken word, a baby who signs loves to label things with the sign.

FIGURE 18–1 *Hug*

HUG

The sign for HUG, as shown in **FIGURE 18–1**, is made by simply giving yourself a hug.

1. **Cross your arms over your chest.**
2. **Grasp your upper arms, squeezing tightly as if hugging.**

You may find that your baby enjoys this newfound ability to embrace himself, and he may do it frequently. If, after he forms the sign, you offer him a hug and he rejects it, it is safe to assume that he is just having fun with the sign. However, it is still important to try to hug him when he makes the sign to continue to reinforce its meaning.

KISS

The sign for KISS (**☉ SEE DVD**) is almost identical to the sign for HOME. KISS is different in that your fingers should be flat across instead of bunched up.

1. **Draw the tips of your fingers and thumb together as if operating a hand puppet with its mouth closed. Fingers should be flat.**

2. Touch all of your fingertips to your lips.
3. Move your fingers up to your cheek, almost as if you are placing a kiss on your cheek from your own lips.

In addition, because this sign starts out in much the same way as EAT, your baby may occasionally mistake one for the other. To help avoid this problem, be sure that the sign for EAT is well established before introducing the sign for KISS. If you are unsure of which sign he is indicating, try giving him a kiss. If that doesn't placate him, he may very well be ready to eat.

E-ALERT

Some babies will get jealous when they see their parents kissing or embracing. If your little one is the jealous type, you may find that he is hesitant to form the signs for KISS and HUG because he doesn't want to give you and your partner any ideas.

If your baby already knows how to kiss or blow kisses, introducing him to this sign will be much easier. Each time he offers you a kiss, form the sign and say the word. Likewise, whenever he sees others kissing, again form the sign and say the word. This may become something of a game for him, leading him to learn the sign quickly.

I LOVE YOU

The sign for I LOVE YOU, as shown in **FIGURE 18-2**, is one that is familiar to many people.

FIGURE 18-2 *I Love You*

1. Hold up your hand, palm facing outward.
2. Extend your thumb, index, and pinky fingers (your middle and ring fingers should remain folded down onto your palm).
3. Shake your hand slightly.

CHAPTER 18

While this is a familiar and well-understood sign to many children and adults, babies and toddlers may have some difficulty forming the sign at first due to the dexterity that it requires. Just continue to model the sign when saying "I love you" and eventually, your child will acquire it.

It is also worth noting that the sign for I LOVE YOU and the sign for AIRPLANE (see Chapter 16) are almost identical. So if you think your child is signing I LOVE YOU, just be on the lookout for an airplane.

HAPPY SIGNS

As a parent, is there anything you find more wonderful than a happy baby? Babies coo, giggle, and squeal to express their joy, and they will also undoubtedly delight in using these signs of happiness. In addition to demonstrating these signs to your baby when they are happy, be sure to model them to express your own happiness, too. This will help to reinforce the meaning of these new signs.

HAPPY

Oddly enough, you may find that the sign for HAPPY (**O SEE DVD**) resembles a general indication of heartburn or an upset stomach.

1. **Place your hand, palm down, on your chest.**
2. **Motion up on your chest with your hand, as if you are showing something coming back up.**

It is acceptable to form this sign with either one or both of your hands.

Because "happy" is a concept and not a tangible object, it will be necessary to find creative ways to demonstrate the sign so that your baby will comprehend it. Particularly effective moments to model this sign include times when your baby squeals in delight, whenever either of you smiles broadly and suddenly, and while doing something that makes your baby especially happy.

E-FACT

The actual American Sign Language sign for STOMACHACHE is formed by holding both of your hands in front of your stomach with the middle fingers of each hand pointed at one another. The middle fingers then twist in opposite directions to indicate pain or discomfort.

LAUGH

The sign for LAUGH is shown in **FIGURE 18-3**.

1. **Form the L hand shape with both hands.**
2. **Point to the corners of your mouth with your index fingers.**
3. **Gesture upward as if indicating a smile, and be sure to smile while you are doing it.**

Many babies and toddlers quickly learn that the act of laughing is one that provokes a positive reaction from adults. Many will then start to offer up fake laughs in order to get that same reaction. If your baby does this, it should be quite easy to get him to use the sign for LAUGH. Simply laugh and form the sign. If he laughs in response (real or fake), make the sign again. Keep playing this back and forth game, and soon he will be signing while he's laughing.

FIGURE 18-3 *Laugh*

SIGNS FOR HIGH SPIRITS

This is another set of signs that indicate good feelings. Your baby may have trouble differentiating between the concepts of each feeling. Because of this, you may want to introduce one sign now and wait on the other. You could also wait until your child is a bit older before introducing either of these signs.

Once your baby does acquire one or both of these signs, you may find that he uses them frequently. This is because the feeling associated with them is a fun one, and he will enjoy expressing that as much as possible. The signs themselves (particularly the sign SURPRISED) are also fun, and your baby will probably like forming them.

E-ALERT

Both "excited" and "surprised" are feelings that your baby could possibly associate with being startled or agitated. Therefore, be sure that when you model the signs, you do so in such a way that your baby can clearly see that you are happy and not upset.

EXCITED

The sign for EXCITED (**◉ SEE DVD**) may at first be difficult because of the dexterity it involves.

1. Spread open your hands and position them in front of your chest.
2. Bend your middle fingers inward so that they are pointed toward you.
3. Motion upward, alternating hands, almost as if brushing something off of your chest with your middle fingers.

If your baby already makes gestures when he is excited, you can use his gestures to help him to understand the sign.

For instance, if your baby jumps or bounces up and down when he is excited, then you should jump or bounce while making the sign. He will eventually put the two together and understand the meaning of the sign.

SURPRISED

The sign for SURPRISED, as shown in **FIGURES 18–4 AND 18–5**, is best modeled using facial expressions in addition to hand motions.

1. **Pinch your index fingers and thumbs together and hold slightly in front of your face by the corners of your eyes.**
2. **Quickly open the pinched digits wide as if indicating wide-eyed surprise.**

FIGURE 18–4 *Surprised (Step One)*

> ### E-SSENTIAL
>
> Many American Sign Language signs rely on facial expressions to provide emphasis. Therefore, it is important to incorporate these facial expressions into the signs for feelings. For instance, you can assume a wide-eyed look when signing SURPRISED, frown when signing SAD, and smile when signing HAPPY or LAUGH.

If your baby likes to try to startle you by "sneaking" up on you or saying "boo," then you will have many opportunities to demonstrate SURPRISE. Another good time is when you and your baby are playing peek-a-boo type games. For example, "hide" behind a piece of furniture or doorway, making sure that your child can still see you. When he excitedly finds you (as he undoubtedly will), form the sign for SURPRISE.

During your attempts to demonstrate this sign, be careful not to startle your baby. If he is easily frightened, sudden surprises may be unpleasant for him. As a result, he could end up associating the sign for SURPRISE with negative experiences.

FIGURE 18–5 *Surprised (Step Two)*

DOWN-AND-OUT SIGNS

Unfortunately, not all feelings are pleasant ones. Your baby is undoubtedly familiar with these unhappy feelings but probably has no way (other than crying) to express them. This inability to communicate can lead to further sadness and frustration. The signs in this section will give him the tools he needs to express himself, even when he is feeling down.

FIGURE 18–6 *Cry*

CRY

The sign for CRY, as shown in **FIGURE 18–6**, is simple to form and is a good representation of the word.

1. Touch the tips of your index fingers just under your eyes.
2. Move your fingers downward to indicate tears.

As simple as this sign is, and as many opportunities as you will undoubtedly have to demonstrate it, CRY can still be a difficult sign for babies to demonstrate. Why? Most likely because when they are crying, they are preoccupied with the cause of their distress and have no inclination to focus on the sign that you are so diligently modeling.

One way to overcome this distraction is to wait until your baby has stopped crying. Touch his tears and then form the sign. He may begin to associate tears with the sign for CRY. Also, be sure to demonstrate the sign whenever your baby witnesses anyone else crying.

SAD

The sign for SAD (**○ SEE DVD**) is another good representation of the feeling it illustrates.

1. **Hold your open hands in front of your face with your palms facing you.**
2. **Bring your hands downward, tilting your head down slightly as you do.**

This motion, coupled with an appropriate facial expression, gives the appearance of sadness.

E-FACT

In order to express extreme sadness, users of American Sign Language will sometimes spell out the word "sad," using the manual alphabet. Likewise, one could spell out "mad" to indicate profound anger. Signing a word in this way is equivalent to adding the word "very" before the feeling.

Another concept sign, SAD may take a while for your baby to acquire. You will, of course, have to look for opportunities when your child is sad, but he may not make the connection right away. For instance, if he is sad because he can't have another cracker, then he might associate the sign with not getting another cracker—until the next time you form it, at which time he may associate it with having to take a nap, or come in from outdoors, or whatever else is making him unhappy. Just remember to say the word every time you sign it, and be sure to have a sad look on your face. This will help him to understand.

CHAPTER 18

SIGNS OF NERVOUSNESS

Even the most fearless of babies get scared sometimes. Some babies are startled by loud noises, while others are terrified of strangers. It is important to take your child's fears seriously and never ridicule him because of them. Remember that babies go through phases of uncertainty; in time, he will outgrow many of his fears. In the meantime, he will be able to express his fears by using the signs in this section, giving you the opportunity to acknowledge them and to help him through them.

AFRAID

Form the sign for AFRAID (**● SEE DVD**) like so.

1. Curl your hands into fists.
2. Move your hands in front of your body, opening them wide as you do. It should look like you are shielding your chest with your hands.

You will probably find that it is most effective to model this sign during times when your child is wary of something, rather than actually afraid of it. When he is scared, he will not be able to focus on a sign. Likewise, you will probably be too busy comforting him to bother with signing. When your child sees or hears something that he is mildly wary of, he will be better able to pay attention to the sign.

FIGURE 18–7 *Shy*

SHY

Though it may take a while for your baby to be able to label his shyness, learning the sign for SHY, as shown in **FIGURE 18–7**, will help tremendously when he does.

1. Brush your cheek with the back of your fingers.
2. At the same time, tilt your head to the side slightly.

Babies and toddlers are notorious for hiding behind a parent's leg when they feel shy. This is the perfect opportunity to model this sign. Simply bend down, form the sign, and say the word. It may take a little time, but he will start to connect the feeling with the sign.

SIGNS OF TEMPER

Temper, temper! The older and more independent your child gets, the more he will display his temper. Fortunately for you, your baby is a signer and will probably have fewer temper tantrums than his nonsigning peers. This is not to say that he won't ever get angry or upset because of course he will. That is where the signs in this section will come in handy.

The signs for ANGRY and for MAD can be used interchangeably, but both are included here so that you can pick the one that you think will be easiest for your child to form and remember. It is not necessary to use both with your child. There is no point in introducing signs he can't use, nor do you want to confuse him with multiple signs for the same word.

E-ALERT

It isn't only growing independence that leads to temper tantrums in a toddler. Boredom, tiredness, and hunger can all bring out the monster in your little one. Trying to head off these problems before they arise may help to reduce temper tantrums in your child.

ANGRY

The sign for ANGRY, as shown in **FIGURE 18–8**, is another sign that benefits from the use of facial expressions.

1. **Hold your hand, palm toward you, in front of your face and bend your fingers in.**
2. **Pull your hand away while making an angry facial expression.**

FIGURE 18–8 *Angry*

To demonstrate this sign, wait for indications that your child is angry, such as when he does not get his way. If he is too angry, of course, he will be unable to focus on the sign, so try to wait until he has calmed down a bit.

MAD

As with ANGRY, timing is everything when it comes to modeling the sign for MAD (**⊙ SEE DVD**). Wait for the right moments, and then try to capture your baby's attention.

1. Bend your fingers as if they were claws.
2. "Scratch" upward on your torso.

This may be the easier sign for your child to form; however, it might remind your child of the sign for BEAR (page 87). Be sure that your baby has one completely established before introducing the other.

Chapter 19

Troubleshooting Common Problems

When your baby is learning to walk, you can expect that she will fall on her diaper-padded bottom many times. You will not be able to prevent it from happening, but knowing that a fall is inevitable will make you better prepared to handle it when it does happen. Likewise, your baby will have many "stumbles" as she acquires the language of sign. Find out about these common signing problems so that you can be prepared when they occur.

19

Baby Isn't Paying Attention

Babies are busy creatures. They are constantly checking out the world around them and learning all sorts of new things. They have very short attention spans and are not likely to focus on any given thing for very long. For that reason, you may find that it is sometimes difficult to get your baby to pay attention to your signing efforts.

Unfortunately, there is no way to force your baby to watch you as you sign. The good news is that you are not missing out on valuable learning time when your baby is unfocused because babies absorb the most information when they are in a state of quiet attentiveness. It is important to watch for these moments of attentiveness in your child. So, for example, if she is not paying attention at the start of her feeding, when you would normally demonstrate the sign, perhaps she will be attentive by the middle or the end of it. If so, use that opportunity to demonstrate the sign. If your baby goes through the entire feeding and doesn't gaze at you for more than a moment at a time, just wait until the next feeding. You will eventually find a time when your baby is attentive and alert and therefore ready to participate.

Baby Won't Sign

When you first set out to sign with your baby, you may be filled with visions of carrying on fluent conversations with your infant. After a couple of weeks of signing with no reaction from your baby at all, you may find yourself disappointed and convinced that your baby will never sign.

Remember that even under the best of circumstances, it still takes time for a baby to sign. You may have begun signing at just the right stage in your baby's development. You may have started with the perfect first signs. You may demonstrate the signs every time the opportunity arises. Even still, it may be weeks or months before your baby offers you a sign in return.

It is understandable that as time wears on, you may begin to grow discouraged. This is the plight of signing parents everywhere. Talk to other signing parents for support and encouragement. Continue to follow the suggestions given in this book, and seek out as many opportunities to sign as possible. As with any other skill your baby has yet to master, this one will take time. Be patient and diligent, and soon your baby will be signing.

> ## E-FACT
>
> Some babies begin walking as early as nine months. Others walk as late as eighteen months. Both of these extremes are considered to be normal. In the same way, some babies will begin forming their first signs in just a couple of weeks, while others may take a few months.

Is Baby Really Signing?

After you have begun to sign with your baby, you may find that she is making new and unusual gestures that you never noticed before. They don't *quite* look like the signs you have used with her, though you must admit there may be a slight resemblance. You begin to experience the first stirrings of hope and you think that maybe, just maybe, your baby is signing.

Just a Coincidence?

As the parent of a baby, you have likely witnessed your child as she tries out her new body, checking to see what it can do. Younger infants, especially, will sometimes test their range of motion by stretching, wiggling, and flexing their limbs. It is for that reason that you may have trouble believing that your child is actually signing. You may worry that you will interpret her spontaneous movements as a deliberate sign.

The good news is that your baby probably *is* signing. At the very least, she is likely trying to imitate the gestures she has watched you make, even if she has yet to comprehend their meanings.

It is better to give her the benefit of the doubt and react as if you are sure she is deliberately communicating with you. Acknowledge the sign, and then give her what you think she may be asking for. If she *is* signing, then you will be showing her that signing is a form of communication. If she is not signing, she may still associate the gestures with getting something she wants. This will take her one step closer to actually signing. And if it turns out that she didn't want the object you thought she was asking for, she will undoubtedly let you know it!

E-ALERT

Be on the lookout for vague movements that resemble a sign. For example, the sign for EAT requires that you bring the tips of your fingers up to your lips and tap twice. Initially, though, your baby might simply bring her entire hand to her mouth. Even without the finger movements, she is still signing.

Handling Early Signs

Because your baby's first signs are likely quite different than their true American Sign Language (ASL) counterparts, you will have to decide if you will encourage the true sign or your baby's version. If you are encouraging modified signs, then you can choose to adopt your baby's adaptation of the sign as the one you will continue to use. Simply begin modeling her version of the sign each time you make it. If you want to adhere to actual ASL signs, however, then continue to model the ASL sign, while still acknowledging and responding to her sign. With enough repetition, your baby's signs will become more and more accurate. They may never be done with the accuracy of an adult, but they will get better and easier to understand.

Baby Is Making Up Her Own Signs

You feel certain that your baby is actually trying to sign, but now it seems as if she is making up her own signs. This is not only possible but likely. Babies have a natural inclination to gesture to get what they want. Even babies who do not learn to sign quickly figure out that they can lift their arms to be picked up or point to an object they want. A baby who signs is even more aware of the possibilities that gesturing offers her. She is likely to form all sorts of gestures to get her needs met.

As with a baby's variations on ASL, the way you use (or choose not to use) these homemade gestures depends on the school of sign you are using. If you are using home signs or modified sign language, then these gestures will fit right into your plan of instruction. If you are strictly adhering to ASL, just continue to demonstrate the ASL signs, and your baby will acquire them in time.

E-FACT

Some babies begin to demonstrate their own gestures as early as six months of age, though many will not actively gesture until they are nine months old or older. Gestures that you may see your baby develop on her own include pointing, waving, and clapping.

No One Else Will Participate

You have explained all the benefits. You have shown everyone how easy it can be. Still, though, you can't get your spouse or relatives or child's caregiver to participate. Is it time to throw in the towel?

Not at all. Even babies who only have one person in their lives who signs with them can still benefit greatly. It may require more effort on your part if you are the sole signer, but your child can still acquire all the signs you want her to use. She may be slower to acquire some signs, especially if she spends a great deal of time with other people, but the signs will come. Look for as many opportunities as you can to demonstrate each sign you are introducing to her.

E-SSENTIAL

Even if the other adults in your household do not sign with your baby, the other children (if you have any) will probably be eager to. Try to recruit your baby's siblings as your partners in sign, and soon you will all be signing together. Who knows? That may be the motivation your spouse needs to join in.

Many relatives and caregivers are reluctant to practice baby sign language because they are skeptical of its merits and they doubt it can actually be taught. If the other adults in your baby's life share these doubts, they are likely to get excited and jump on board when they see your baby communicating through sign.

Baby's Signs Are Indecipherable

She tries and tries and tries to mimic your signs, but you just aren't sure what your baby is saying. Or perhaps she has two or three signs that resemble each other so much that you never know for sure which one she is using. These are common problems in signing families and are almost unavoidable. There are a few things you can do, however, to help translate your baby's signs:

- **Consider the context of the sign.** What is going on in baby's environment? What time of day is it? For example, if it is mealtime and others are eating, your baby might be trying to make the sign for EAT.
- **Watch for visual clues.** Is your baby doing anything else that would indicate her wants or needs? A baby who is alternating signing with rubbing her eyes is possibly trying to indicate sleep. One who is signing and pointing at the refrigerator may be asking for juice.
- **Avoid using like signs.** In the beginning, try to avoid using signs with your baby that closely resemble each other, such as MORE and BALL. This will reduce potential confusion for both of you.
- **Ask for verbal verification of the sign.** Babies often understand a spoken word long before they are able to say it. So if you think you know what your baby might be signing, just ask. An excited reaction is a good indication that you've interpreted correctly.

The longer your baby signs, the better she will become at forming the signs correctly. Likewise, the more you read her signs, the easier it will become for you. You will learn to interpret the little nuances that make her signs different from the standard formations. Just as you may have to work especially hard to understand your child's speech when she learns to talk, it will take some time to understand her hand speak when she learns to sign.

Baby Is "Forgetting" Some Signs

Your baby has been signing for weeks and has a growing vocabulary of signs. Suddenly, though, you notice that she is neglecting to use some of the signs she has been using since the beginning. It is as if she has forgotten some of her first signs.

The reality is that once your baby has learned a sign, she is unlikely to forget it as long as you continue to demonstrate it each time you use the word. Instead, she is probably dropping a sign temporarily so that she may turn her attention to other signs. Babies commonly do this as they learn any number of new skills. For instance, a baby may stop waving when she begins clapping. Or she may stop saying "da da" when she learns to say "ma ma." But these skills are not lost. Instead, a baby will pick up the old skill again after she has mastered the new one. In the same way, with continued encouragement, your baby will probably resume using her earlier signs.

E-ALERT

Occasionally, you may encounter a sign that your baby rarely needs and therefore has trouble remembering. You may want to then consider whether the sign is one that your baby actually needs in her vocabulary. If not, perhaps you should introduce other signs that she will be more likely to use.

As she grows more comfortable with her expanding repertoire of signs, your baby will eventually start using the old signs again. You can ensure that she does not forget the signs by continuing to model them in her presence, even if she fails to do so. This will keep the signs fresh in her memory, and she will pick them back up before long.

You Are Forgetting Some Signs

You have been practicing sign language with your child for a while and have developed a signing vocabulary of twenty, thirty, or fifty or more signs. Suddenly you find that you are losing track of which signs are which, particularly those you introduced in the beginning. If you have been consistent in demonstrating the signs both old and new, you probably won't have too much trouble remembering them. A memory lapse can happen occasionally, though, and so it is a good idea to have your signs organized for your reference.

One way to keep track of the signs you have taught is to keep a log. This can be a notebook where you jot down signs you have taught, a photo album with pictures of you or your baby forming the signs, or simply a book (such as this one) where you have marked each sign as you have taught it. For more ideas on documenting your baby's signing progress, see Chapter 20.

Another way to keep from forgetting the signs is by keeping a reference sheet with you. Simply write out instructions for forming signs you most commonly use with your baby and tuck it into your purse or wallet. Then, no matter where you are, you will have your signs with you.

Baby Has Begun Speaking

If your baby is beginning to talk, you may be wondering if you should continue to sign with her. The primary purpose of baby sign language, after all, is to give babies a way to communicate *before* they are able to speak. You may have also found that your baby is less likely to work at signing now that she is speaking. In spite of these things, there are still compelling reasons to continue signing.

Signing Beyond the Basics

If your child is beginning to use simple words to get her needs met, she will have less motivation to learn new signs. In fact, many parents opt to stop signing as their children start speaking. Remember, though, that even a toddler who is learning to talk still has trouble communicating some thoughts and desires. Using sign language, even as she acquires verbal skills, will help to bridge that communication gap until she is more proficient in her speech and better able to express herself. Likewise, if your baby is starting to talk *before* you have begun sign language instruction, you can use signs to help your baby express words that she cannot yet say.

E-SSENTIAL

Not only will she hesitate to learn new signs, you may also find that your baby begins to drop some well-established signs as she replaces them with the spoken word. If you want to maintain her signing vocabulary, continue to model the signs even when she doesn't. Otherwise, she will start to forget them.

Even after your baby begins to talk, remember to speak each word as you or your baby signs it. This will help to improve her growing spoken vocabulary and will also help her to make a connection between a verbal word and a sign. You may find that in time, your baby begins to speak and sign some words simultaneously. This is the best indication of total comprehension.

A Foundation for the Future

As you have read, many parents introduce sign language to give their children a foundation for a second language. If this benefit of baby sign language is important to you, you certainly will not want to quit signing with your baby as soon as she begins to talk.

Instead, you may want to take this opportunity to start introducing more advanced signs to your toddler. These signs could include those that are more difficult to form or that represent intangible concepts. This will enable her to communicate beyond her basic needs and give her a larger vocabulary of signs.

As she gets older and is ready to learn fluent American Sign Language, her large and well-established vocabulary of signs will give her a head start on the language. This will make fluent signing easier for her to achieve and more enjoyable for her to learn.

Chapter 20

Now That Baby Is Signing

After weeks or months during which you have diligently demonstrated sign after sign, your baby is finally getting the hang of it. He is beginning to use signs to make his desires known, and he readily responds to your signs. So where do you go from here? In this chapter, find out what to expect now that your baby is signing and read up on tips for making signing fun and easy for you and your baby.

20

Understanding "Baby Dialect"

While signing with your baby, you have undoubtedly had a bit of trouble from time to time understanding what he is signing. Throughout this book, you have read about ways to overcome this common communication gap. Now that he has reached the point where he is signing frequently and consistently, however, you are probably expecting that translation should be easy.

Over time, your baby's signs *will* become easier to decipher. Compare the accuracy of his very first signs to the accuracy of his later signs. It has most certainly improved noticeably. However, it is important to realize that while he is a baby or young toddler, your child will likely never sign with the accuracy of an adult. Therefore, you will have to learn to understand this signing "dialect" that your baby uses. Here are some ways in which a baby's signs may be different from their American Sign Language counterparts:

- **Lack of repetition:** Some signs require a repetitive motion that babies will neglect to make. The sign for BEAR, for instance, is made by clawing at your chest repeatedly. Your baby, however, may simply grab at his chest to indicate this sign.
- **Too much repetition:** Alternatively, babies will sometimes repeat a motion more times than is necessary. For example, the sign for CHILD requires that you pat the air in front of you twice. Your baby may pat it over and over, giving the appearance of waving his hand wildly.
- **Fingerless signs:** Many signs that require complex finger maneuvers may be too difficult for your baby to sign. The sign for I LOVE YOU is made by extending your thumb, index, and pinky fingers. Your baby may be unable to do this and may therefore omit one or more fingers from the sign.
- **Improper positioning:** When a baby practices a sign, he focuses primarily on the hand motion and less on the placement of that hand. So, for example, he may not form the sign for DIAPER at his waist (where the sign should be formed), but instead, he may make the pinching motion in the air.

As your baby becomes more proficient at signing, you will probably see a pattern in the way he signs. You will recognize his modifications, and you will not have to work so hard to figure out what he is trying to tell you. Over time, his signs will also become more accurate, and you will not have to translate his unique dialect nearly as much.

Give Him What He Wants

By now, your baby has likely figured out that signing is a good way to ask for what he wants. So what is the most effective way to keep him signing? Keep giving him what he wants. Of course, there are limits to what you can freely give your baby, but when it is possible, respond quickly and affirmatively to his signs. It should not be surprising that your child may try to take advantage of your quick response. If you are unable to give him what he is asking for, be sure to acknowledge the sign anyway. For example, if your child wants another cookie, you can say, "I know that you want another cookie, but you can't have one right now." You might then follow that statement with the sign for ALL GONE. Don't be surprised, however, if he throws a temper tantrum at your refusal to honor his request. He is just learning to express himself and will probably become extremely frustrated when this new form of communication doesn't get him what he wants. Whether this happens or not, try to distract your child so that he does not dwell on what he didn't get.

E-ALERT

Even if the rest of your family is not signing with your baby, showing them these early signs is so important. If your baby signs to his other parent or sibling and does not get a response, he may get discouraged, which could slow his signing progress.

As time goes on and your child becomes more proficient in his signing abilities, a quick response will be less necessary than it is in the beginning. This is because he has confidence in his ability to communicate. He will know with certainty that you understand his signs and he will keep signing, even if he doesn't get what he wants every single time. Do still try to respond as quickly as you can, but don't despair over lost opportunities.

Keep It Simple, Keep It Fun

The most successful signers are the children whose parents seamlessly incorporate signing into their everyday lives. These babies are exposed to signing in a frequent and casual way, making it a natural part of their lives. Not only does this make it easier for your baby, but taking a fun and casual approach will make it easier for you, too. The easiest habits to get into are the ones that fit neatly into our lives with little effort. For signing to be successful, it will have to become a habit. Therefore, try to make it easy on yourself.

Signing Is Not a Chore

Signing should never be something that you or your baby dreads, nor should it ever seem like work. Instead, signing should be a pleasure for you and your child. If you find that you are working hard at showing your child how to sign, you are probably trying harder than you need to. Once you have learned a sign yourself, the work is basically over. After that, just demonstrate the sign each time the opportunity arises. It is not necessary to make a big deal of it, nor is it necessary to spend extended periods of time modeling the sign.

> **E-SSENTIAL**
>
> A great way to pick up a few new signs without putting much thought or effort into it is by watching a signing video or DVD. You don't even have to put your full attention into it. Let it play while you are tidying up or doing laundry or some other menial task, and you will end up learning a few new signs while you're at it.

Keep in mind that your child will be learning new signs at a relatively slow pace, meaning there is no reason for you to learn dozens of signs all at once. Learn a few here and a few there in your spare time. As you practice them with your baby, they will become more familiar to you, and you will no longer have to think about them.

It is also worth noting that the more people who are signing with your baby, the easier signs will be for you to remember. This is because you will be exposed to the signs over and over again as the other people in your baby's life form them. This will act as a constant reminder for you of your baby's most commonly used signs.

Signing Games

One way to ensure that your signing efforts are more fun than work is to make a game out of them. Games for babies are usually more flexible than structured and may evolve as you play them. When playing a game with your little one, try to let him take the lead.

One activity to help your child learn to sign is based on two essential baby premises. First, babies love it when adults are silly, and second, babies love to imitate. When your baby sees an object of interest and gazes at it or points it out to you, form the sign while you get really silly or excited. Your baby will get a kick out of your excitement and will probably attempt to imitate you. As always, pile on the praise when your baby signs.

You could also try incorporating your baby's toys into signing games. For example, if your baby is currently learning animal signs, pull out the stuffed animals. Hide them behind your back and pull out one at a time. Each time you reveal an animal, form the corresponding sign. It probably will not take long until he is forming the sign before you have a chance.

E-QUESTION

What if my baby thinks signing is just a game?

If you only exposed him to signs while playing games, he probably would. But you will be demonstrating these signs during *all* of your day-to-day activities, including games, and he will learn that signing is a form of communication.

Another fun activity is to sign while singing. Sing your baby's favorite songs and add in the appropriate signs. For example, if your baby loves "The Wheels on the Bus," learn the signs for BUS, WHEEL, BABY, HORN, and other key words in the song. Start using them instead of the traditional hand motions for the song. This is an excellent way to keep your baby's attention while signing.

Finally, if your baby is learning signs for the people in his life, pull out the photo albums. Your baby will enjoy looking at pictures of familiar faces, and you can take the opportunity to form the sign for each person in the photos.

Signing Spurts

If it seems like "Be patient" is the signing parent's mantra, take heart, for there is some good news. In the same way that children will go through periodic physical growth spurts, signing babies will usually hit a signing spurt. At some point, your child will begin to associate signing with communication. He will see that for every sign he forms, he can expect a favorable reaction from you. When this knowledge clicks in his mind, he will very likely pick up a number of new signs, seemingly overnight. He may go from a vocabulary of a handful of signs to a vocabulary of dozens of signs in just a few days.

E-FACT

A baby who has been consistently exposed to sign language from seven or eight months of age could easily have a signing vocabulary of twenty to thirty words by the time he is one year old! This extensive vocabulary will continue to grow as long as you continue to introduce new signs.

When this happens (and it usually does), it will be especially important to continue to model your child's earliest signs. It is natural to want to focus on all of the new signs your baby is learning, but he will forget the earliest signs if they are not maintained. It will also be especially important for you to keep everybody in your baby's life updated on his rapidly changing signing abilities.

Keep Track of Baby's Signs

As your baby learns more and more signs, you will probably want to document them in some way. There are two reasons for this. First, documenting each sign your baby has learned will help *you* to remember them. Secondly, it is a nice way to showcase your child's achievements. There are several tried-and-true methods of recording baby signs, but use whatever method is easiest and most preferable to you. It is not necessary to spend a lot of time or money on your log. If you remember to keep it simple and organized, you will likely be pleased with the results.

Signing Journals

Many parents keep a journal for their babies anyway. If this is something that you do already, it should be easy to get into the habit of recording your baby's signing adventures. If you are not already a journalist, it is easy to begin. The hardest part about it is remembering to do it on a regular basis.

First you will need to get a journal. It can be anything from a cheap spiral-bound notebook to a fancy leather-bound blank book. Then, every time you introduce a sign, write about it in your journal. Name the sign and how it is formed, as well as any reaction from your baby. Likewise, when your baby first forms a sign on his own, be sure to write about that milestone. In the years to come, you will be glad to have a well-documented account of your baby's jaunt into the world of sign.

Photo Albums

A photo album or scrapbook is a nice way to document your baby's signing journey and will be a memento that you can keep forever. You, your child, and other loved ones will enjoy looking at these photos for years to come. The only drawback to a photo album is that you have to wait until your child is proficient at a sign before you can expect him to model it for the camera. For this reason, a photo album is not a good record of the signs that your baby is only starting to demonstrate. It is mainly a nice keepsake for after the fact. Therefore, if you do opt to keep a photo album of your baby's signs, it is probably a good idea to keep a written record somewhere, too. That way, you will have an easily accessible reference for yourself until the photo album is complete.

E-ALERT

If you choose to mount your photographs in a scrapbook, be sure to use only acid-free and lignin-free papers to keep your photos safe. Lignin can cause a chemical breakdown of your photos, while acid can cause them to become brittle and discolored. Most craft stores carry an extensive assortment of photo-safe papers.

For ease of organization, consider grouping your photographs by category of signs (such as food signs, clothing signs, outdoor signs, and so on) or chronologically in the order your baby learned them. If you are using the album as a reference for yourself or someone else, organizing the photos by category is probably your best option. If, however, you are creating a keepsake for yourself, then you will likely want the photos in chronological order.

Video Diary

If you have a camcorder at your disposal, a video diary is a fun way to record your baby as he learns to sign. When you are prepared to introduce a new sign, simply set up the camera and let it run as you model the new sign. Later, when your baby begins signing back, you will want to record those moments, as well. Your baby's loved ones will undoubtedly enjoy watching your baby as he acquires this new skill.

The problem with a video diary, however, is that it is easy to miss those early signs because they sometimes just appear out of nowhere and without warning. You may find that you are only able to capture a sign once your baby has started to regularly use it. To increase the chances of capturing your baby's first signs on video, be sure to have your camera ready whenever your baby is in a situation where he is likely to sign. For instance, if you are using the sign for EAT, have the camera rolling every time you put him in his high chair. If nothing else, you may end up with a recording of your baby tossing his bowl off of the tray or smearing food on his face— footage that Grandma will undoubtedly find adorable!

Signing Log

A quick and easy way to keep track of your baby's signs is to create a signing log. A blank log is provided in Appendix B of this book, but you can develop any system that works for you. The basics of the signing log should include the name of the sign, the date it was introduced, the date your baby first signed or responded to it, a description of the sign, and possibly any other notes of importance.

E-FACT

There are many words that have more than one corresponding American Sign Language sign. For example, there are at least three acceptable ways to sign MAN. For future reference, a detailed description of each sign is a must in your signing log. That way there will never be confusion as to which version of a sign you used.

You can make your signing log a little more special by putting it in a pretty book, scrapbook, or journal and attaching photos of your baby forming the signs. This will give you an easy reference, as well as a keepsake of this time in your baby's life.

Enjoy Speaking with Your Baby

After months of effort, you are finally able to communicate with your baby in a way that would not have been possible without the use of sign. He is sharing with you his wants, feelings, and observations in a way that not all babies can. And while his signing is bridging the existing communication gap, it won't be long before your baby begins to speak. You may find that you have bittersweet feelings as he learns to talk.

Every milestone in your child's life and every stage in his development are beautiful and exciting moments that should be treasured. This time of personal and intimate conversation, however, may be especially poignant to a parent. After all, you are connecting with your child in a very deep way, and you have worked hard to get your child to this point. When he begins to talk, his signing days may be over.

E-SSENTIAL

Babies will naturally drop their signs as they learn to speak. However, if you want your child to continue signing into toddlerhood and childhood, just keep signing. As long as you do not stop modeling the sign when you or he says a word, he is likely to continue to enjoy communicating through signing.

When your little one does learn to talk, you will begin a whole new adventure in communication. You will delight in listening to him as he chatters about anything and everything, and the two of you will enjoy new realms of communication. However, you may find that you still miss the days of signing with your baby. So be sure to enjoy this very special time and the intimate conversation that you share exclusively with your baby.

Appendix A

Baby Signing Resources

SIGN LANGUAGE WEB SITES

ASL Pro
✎*www.aslpro.com*
This site offers a free comprehensive ASL video dictionary.

ASL University
✎*www.lifeprint.com*
This site is a great resource that includes an expansive ASL dictionary, free online lessons, and information on Deaf culture.

Baby Hands Productions
✎*www.mybabycantalk.com*
Although this Web site sells baby sign-language products, it also offers a number of free resources including a video dictionary and tips on signing with your baby.

Signing with Your Baby
✎*www.signingbaby.com*
This is an informative Web site written and maintained by a signing mother.

SUGGESTED READING FOR SIGNING PARENTS

Acredolo, Linda, Susan Goodwyn, and Douglas Abrams. *Baby Signs: How to Talk with Your Baby Before Your Baby Can Talk*. (New York, NY: McGraw-Hill, 2002).

This classic guide to baby sign language primarily advocates baby gestures, though the updated version includes a number of ASL signs, as well.

Garcia, Joseph. *Sign with Your Baby: How to Communicate with Infants Before They Can Speak*. (Seattle, WA: Northlight Communications, 1999).

Written by a pioneer in the field of baby sign language, this book is one of the original how-to guides on the subject.

STORYBOOKS FOR SIGNING BABIES AND TODDLERS

Ault, Kelly, and Leo Landry. *Let's Sign: Every Baby's Guide to Communicating with Grownups*. (New York, NY: Houghton Mifflin, 2005).

This simple and clearly illustrated book demonstrates signs through the telling of three separate stories.

Breindel, Tina Jo, and Michael Carter. *First Signs*. (San Diego, CA: DawnSign Press, 2006).

This book's bright and silly illustrations appeal to young children and depict some basic, early signs.

Collins, Stanley. *First Signs*. (Eugene, OR: Garlic Press, 2001).

This board book contains both photos and illustrations of some of babies' earliest signs.

Cryan, Michelle. *Where Is Baby?: A Lift-the-Flap Sign Language Book*. (Washington, DC: Gallaudet University Press, 2007).

This interactive book demonstrates and illustrates several highly motivating signs.

Baby Signing Log

SIGN	DATE INTRODUCED	DATE FIRST USED	DESCRIPTION OF SIGN	NOTES

SIGN	DATE INTRODUCED	DATE FIRST USED	DESCRIPTION OF SIGN	NOTES

American Sign Language Manual Alphabet

A	B	C
D	E	F
G	H	I
J	K	L

American Sign Language Manual Alphabet (*continued*)

Y	Z	1
2	3	4
5	6	7
8	9	0

Index

JUN 0 1 2011

YOU SHOULD CAREFULLY READ THE FOLLOWING TERMS AND CONDITIONS BEFORE USING THIS SOFTWARE PRODUCT. INSTALLING AND USING THIS PRODUCT INDICATES YOUR ACCEPTANCE OF THESE CONDITIONS. IF YOU DO NOT AGREE WITH THESE TERMS AND CONDITIONS, DO NOT INSTALL THE SOFTWARE AND RETURN THIS PACKAGE PROMPTLY FOR A FULL REFUND.

1. Grant of License
This software package is protected under United States copyright law and international treaty. You are hereby entitled to one copy of the enclosed software and are allowed by law to make one backup copy or to copy the contents of the disks onto a single hard disk and keep the originals as your backup or archival copy. United States copyright law prohibits you from making a copy of this software for use on any computer other than your own computer. United States copyright law also prohibits you from copying any written material included in this software package without first obtaining the permission of F+W Publications, Inc.

2. Restrictions
You, the end-user, are hereby prohibited from the following:
You may not rent or lease the Software or make copies to rent or lease for profit or for any other purpose.
You may not disassemble or reverse compile for the purposes of reverse engineering the Software.
You may not modify or adapt the Software or documentation in whole or in part, including, but not limited to, translating or creating derivative works.

3. Transfer
You may transfer the Software to another person, provided that (a) you transfer all of the Software and documentation to the same transferee; (b) you do not retain any copies; and (c) the transferee is informed of and agrees to the terms and conditions of this Agreement.

4. Termination
This Agreement and your license to use the Software can be terminated without notice if you fail to comply with any of the provisions set forth in this Agreement. Upon termination of this Agreement, you promise to destroy all copies of the software including backup or archival copies as well as any documentation associated with the Software. All disclaimers of warranties and limitation of liability set forth in this Agreement shall survive any termination of this Agreement.

5. Limited Warranty
F+W Publications, Inc. warrants that the Software will perform according to the manual and other written materials accompanying the Software for a period of 30 days from the date of receipt. F+W Publications, Inc. does not accept responsibility for any malfunctioning computer hardware or any incompatibilities with existing or new computer hardware technology.

6. Customer Remedies
F+W Publications, Inc.'s entire liability and your exclusive remedy shall be, at the option of F+W Publications, Inc., either refund of your purchase price or repair and/or replacement of Software that does not meet this Limited Warranty. Proof of purchase shall be required. This Limited Warranty will be voided if Software failure was caused by abuse, neglect, accident or misapplication. All replacement Software will be warranted based on the remainder of the warranty or the full 30 days, whichever is shorter and will be subject to the terms of the Agreement.

7. No Other Warranties
F+W PUBLICATIONS, INC., TO THE FULLEST EXTENT OF THE LAW, DISCLAIMS ALL OTHER WARRANTIES, OTHER THAN THE LIMITED WARRANTY IN PARAGRAPH 5, EITHER EXPRESS OR IMPLIED, ASSOCIATED WITH ITS SOFTWARE, INCLUDING BUT NOT LIMITED TO IMPLIED WARRANTIES OF MERCHANTABILITY AND FITNESS FOR A PARTICULAR PURPOSE, WITH REGARD TO THE SOFTWARE AND ITS ACCOMPANYING WRITTEN MATERIALS. THIS LIMITED WARRANTY GIVES YOU SPECIFIC LEGAL RIGHTS. DEPENDING UPON WHERE THIS SOFTWARE WAS PURCHASED, YOU MAY HAVE OTHER RIGHTS.

8. Limitations on Remedies
TO THE MAXIMUM EXTENT PERMITTED BY LAW, F+W PUBLICATIONS, INC. SHALL NOT BE HELD LIABLE FOR ANY DAMAGES WHATSO-EVER, INCLUDING WITHOUT LIMITATION, ANY LOSS FROM PERSONAL INJURY, LOSS OF BUSINESS PROFITS, BUSINESS INTERRUPTION, BUSINESS INFORMATION OR ANY OTHER PECUNIARY LOSS ARISING OUT OF THE USE OF THIS SOFTWARE.
This applies even if F+W Publications, Inc. has been advised of the possibility of such damages. F+W Publications, Inc.'s entire liability under any provision of this agreement shall be limited to the amount actually paid by you for the Software. Because some states may not allow for this type of limitation of liability, the above limitation may not apply to you.
THE WARRANTY AND REMEDIES SET FORTH ABOVE ARE EXCLUSIVE AND IN LIEU OF ALL OTHERS, ORAL OR WRITTEN, EXPRESS OR IMPLIED. No F+W Publications, Inc. dealer, distributor, agent, or employee is authorized to make any modification or addition to the warranty.

9. General
This Agreement shall be governed by the laws of the United States of America and the Commonwealth of Massachusetts. If you have any questions concerning this Agreement, contact F+W Publications, Inc., via Adams Media at 508-427-7100. Or write to us at: Adams Media, an F+W Publications Company, 57 Littlefield Street, Avon, MA 02322.